People of Integrity

People of Integrity

WILLIAM B. MORGAN, JR.

DISCIPLESHIP RESOURCES

P.O. BOX 340003 • NASHVILLE, TN 37203-0003
www.discipleshipresources.org

ISBN 978-0-88177-513-6
Library of Congress Control Number 2007942062

DR 513

Dedicated To . . .

my wife Dianne

my Uncle Bobby

and the people of the United Methodist Churches
who have permitted me to be their minister
and have so often ministered to me

TABLE OF CONTENTS

Tithes of Time for Our Lives

> In the beginning was the Word, and the Word was with God, and
> the Word was God. . . . What has come into being in him was life,
> and the life was the light of all people. (John 1:1, 3b-4, NRSV)[1]

Forty days is a sort of "tithe of time." Three hundred sixty-five days in a year. The math is not exact, but it's about a tithe-tenth just the same. Matthew, Mark, and Luke recount how Jesus spent forty days in the wilderness following his baptism fasting and praying, to focus, and clarify his call. In a like manner, church people across the years have considered forty days a goodly time for reflection on and discernment of God's presence and call upon our lives.

The Christian season of Lent—the forty days plus Sundays between Ash Wednesday and Easter—is such a tithe of time observed by many people. Those days often include fasting, disciplined prayer, Bible reading, personal and small group study, and deepened attention to worship. We, of course, are not limited to Lent. We are free to choose any period of time for a season of faith and life discernment.

People who give a tithe of their income find that the planning they do in order to do so causes them to pay closer attention to how they spend the other 90% of their finances. This requires decisions about values, priorities, what's truly important. In a like manner, paying attention to our lives during a tithe of time, such as Lent, enables us to examine and assess the rest of our lives, how we are doing, where we need to hold the course, and where we need to go in new directions.

For Christians, such times are not intended merely to look at life in general, to glean a wise aphorism or two, read yet another self-help psychology, latest fad diet-exercise, or feel-good spirituality book, or jump start those resolutions that were long gone by the time we found the crumbs of New Year confetti behind the sofa. Forty-day spiritual journeys like Lent are occasions to look at our lives in connection and alignment with the living and dying of Jesus Christ. His life is the code, the key, the standard, the plumb line by which we measure a life worth living and dying for.

The church I serve as pastor has focused on what we have called whole life stewardship. A steward is one who takes care of something that belongs to another. For Christians, our lives and all we have are seen as gifts from God. In the deepest sense, all that we are and have belong to this great-generous-mysterious One, who we call God. We often reduce stewardship to what we do with our money. But stewardship is much more. Our United Methodist membership vows ask us for whole life stewardship with the promise to commit our prayers (our spiritual lives), presence (our physical lives), gifts (what we have), and service (what we do) to God. These promises refer not just to the church part of our lives but to all of our lives.

As our congregation went deeper into the stewardship of our lives, the word integrity quickly emerged. Whole life stewardship is a life of integrity. Maybe it's always been this way, but it seems to me that our present time hungers and thirsts for integrity in our leaders and all of our lives more than ever. The Merriam-Webster online dictionary reports that "integrity" was the most looked up word in 2005—edging out runners-up "filibuster," "refugee," and "tsunami." "Firm adherence to a code", "incorruptibility" says MW.[2] Yeah, but that doesn't fully get at the full meaning of the word.

A life of stewardship and integrity is one of alignment and congruence of all our "parts"— spirit, body, possessions, and actions—beyond the compartmentalization we rationalize.

What's more, such life is not something we pull off on our own. In truth, it is a gift, an ability, God gives us and restores to us when we fail or fall short.

So, for a short but significant time, we will explore, and by grace, perhaps experience, integrity more fully than before. There's a quip about preparing for a trip to Europe: lay out the clothes and money you plan to take on the bed. Then half the clothes and double the money! So, here's what I suggest we pack for our journey together:

> A good readable-studyable Bible, preferably the New Revised Standard Version or the New International Version.

> Keep your attention antenna up to what's going on in you and in the world near and far beyond you. "Bible in one hand, the newspaper in the other," theologian Karl Barth said.

> Pack some time to read, reflect, brood, and pray.

> Find some people—friends, new acquaintances, even an enemy or two—and commit to meet together once a week over seven weeks or so.

We will look at some strong currents—distinguishable but never totally separable—that flow together in the bubbly stream of life with Christ and each other:

> Integrity and stewardship of our lives.

> God's grace, definitive in Jesus Christ, but abounding everywhere and permeating everything.

> Our faith and life (theology and ethics, beliefs and actions) as United Methodists.

David Lurie is the central character in Rabbi Chaim Potok's novel "In the Beginning." Lurie becomes a world famous Bible scholar. To do so, as a young man, he had both to claim and cut his ties with the extremely orthodox practices of his family. Reflecting over his life, David recalls getting started at things as a boy, as a student, as a teacher of students, in his undertakings and relationships as an adult. "All beginnings are hard. . . Especially a beginning you make by yourself. That's the hardest beginning of all."[3]

So, in this tithe of time for all of our time, on our own yet together, in the middle and muddle of things, let us begin again. Take a deep breath. Let's go deep and forward.

FOREWORD NOTES

1. All biblical quotations are from the New Revised Standard Version, unless noted as author's paraphrase or translation.
2. Adam Gorlick, "'Integrity' Tops Web Dictionary's Lookups," Associated Press, 12/11/05
3. Chaim Potok, *In the Beginning,* p. 3

Acknowledgments

My mind boggles at the thought of what efforts must go into the production of a large book. In length, this is a small book. Yet it is the result of great effort on the part of many.

My clergy colleagues at Canterbury United Methodist Church gave me the encouragement to refine my rough draft chapters into a coherent book. They wrapped the chapters in study helps and provided a leaders' guide for groups.

Reverend Patsy Carlberg authored the probing spiritual reflection exercises at the end of each chapter.

Reverend Warren Nash did excellent "executive summaries" to focus the reading of each chapter.

Reverend Mikah Hudson chose apt Biblical passages and crafted engaging questions for the chapters.

And Dr. Oliver Clark created a group leaders' guide that will enhance personal or group study. Those study helps can be accessed at www.upperroom.org/bookstore/downloads/peopleofintegrity.pdf.

I can only imagine what Canterbury staff members Laura Dabbs, Brooke Vickers, and Gloria McClendon went through with the word processing, formatting, copying, and citation searches.

Even with all that went before, the actual book in hand is a reality because of the good humor and skill of Discipleship Resources editors George Donigian and Terrie Livaudais.

This book is as good as it is because of the efforts of those named and others unnamed. This book is no better than it is because of me alone.

Bill Morgan
Christ the King, 2007

Chapter One

The Dearth and Rebirth of Integrity

From Atticus to Enron

As a high school freshman, I rode the city bus downtown in Birmingham to the venerable Smith and Hardwick Bookstore to buy a copy of the new book *To Kill a Mockingbird* by Alabama writer (and Methodist) Harper Lee. Now, years later, from time to time, I put the classic movie version of the story into the player to watch it yet again.

Set in 1932 in a small Alabama town, the story's central characters are Atticus Finch, a widower lawyer, and his two children, son Jem and daughter Scout. Racial tension flares in the town when a black man is charged (falsely) for assaulting a white woman. Atticus opens himself to great criticism and pressure from the white connnunity by defending the accused man.

In the movie, Atticus is played by veteran actor Gregory Peck. Though a 1960's production, well into the era of cinemascope color, the movie is filmed in black and white . . . and grays . . . which amplify the life issues being explored.

In one scene, Atticus finds first grader Scout brooding on the front steps. He learns that she has gotten in a scrape at school with kids calling her names

15

because of what her dad is doing. Scout asks her father why he is doing something that makes people so mad at him. Looking and sounding very Gregory Peck-ish, a manly gentleman with a resonant blend of Southern and British accents, Atticus answers:

> "For a number of reasons," said Atticus. "The main one is, if I didn't I couldn't hold up my head in town, I couldn't represent this town in the legislature, I couldn't even tell you or Jem . . . to mind me again."[1]

Atticus is describing and living *integrity*. We speak of integrity as a person operating from firm values, or a state of being whole, undivided. Far from settling the matter, that barely scratches the surface and opens the discussion. Integrity is fundamentally personal, though it extends to the integrity of groups of persons: families, communities, churches, businesses, institutions, governments, and such. Values? Whose values? The white community that assailed Atticus Finch had some "firm values" that clashed with those he embodied. Then, there is the matter of integrity expressing the wholeness, consistency, and genuineness of a person. Yet in a multilayered-complex world, are we driven to an inevitable compartmentalization of our lives and a here-but-not-there application of our values?

These questions are raised here to suggest that an "integrity search" is not for the faint. Integrity is one of those hard to define, even harder to live, realities. Integrity, nevertheless, is one of those core-defining qualities that we know when we see it in people and sorely miss it when we don't.

Another word comes to mind and heart: dearth, *a scarcity that makes more dear*. In the post 9/11 early years of the new century, many make a case for a dearth, if not death, of integrity. In the wake of the accounting misrepresentation and stock manipulation scandals of such corporations as Enron and WorldCom, there is a cloud of bewilderment.

During recent years, the perennial human abuse of the good gift of sexuality has rocked our society not because of what happens in bawdy, so called redlight districts, but what has apparently happened in high and holy places. Presidential and Congressional sexual misconduct has cast a shadow across the often otherwise effective public service records of elected leaders. A critical mass of persons has reported the sexual exploitation of themselves or their family members as youth by a (certainly tiny percentage yet still significant) number of Roman Catholic priests. Though perhaps less publicly known, Protestant and Orthodox circles are far from immune. Few communities are untouched by the infidelity of a respected married clergyperson at some time or another.

The integrity quest and question are hardly new. As a college student in the center of the Vietnam War years, I was in a coming-of-age-generation that saw on one hand the unprecedented questioning of the integrity, honor, and compassion of leaders and those who fought the war by those who protested the war. On the other hand, we witnessed a similarly huge questioning of the integrity, courage, and patriotism of the protestors of the war by its proponents.

The next decade, the '70s, brought us Watergate. I am not sure if anyone ever fully figured out who knew what and when about the botched burglary of the offices of one political party orchestrated by the highest level of leaders in the other party. The causes of what led up to those events and the consequences of what unfolded afterward are still open to discussion. Though it was not the first or last time a president's integrity has been questioned, the trauma of a Presidential resignation in dishonor seems to have created an ongoing hair-trigger readiness to question the integrity of leaders in all fields at the slightest provocation.

Across the '80s, with its array of integrity and honesty questions of government and financial leaders related to such as so-called Iran-gate, Contra-gate, junk bond schemes, and Savings and Loan failures, we arrive at the '90s. In *The Best of Times: The Boom and Bust Years of America Before and After Everything Changed* (earlier subtitled, *America in the Clinton Years*), Haynes Johnson explores such spectacles as the O. J. Simpson trial, the Whitewater Investigation, the Lewinsky-Clinton affair, and Florida presidential election controversy.

Integrity-honesty-ethical issues swirl in those cauldrons. Questions abound. How does race and money affect the way people are treated in our justice system and society? Where is the line between shrewd and crooked business deals? What about the ethics of those investigating the ethics of others? What do the media frenzy and profiteering that go on with our myriad scandals—sexual, celebrity, crime, financial political, and such—say about us all?

Haynes Johnson makes the case that these sensational events "divert attention from the really great episodes of the Nineties, especially two that came into play with tremendous force. One—was the revolution in science, technology, and medicine rapidly changing life on the planet. The other was the growing concentration of great blocs of power through the greatest wave of mergers ever, reshaping the basic economic and social structures of the nation."[2]

In the '90s, the new world of computers and Internet seems to have made changes everywhere. The way business is done. The way governments function. Who has and who doesn't have information. The disparity between haves and have-nots escalate. Genetic research brings huge new value-laden choices to us regarding cloning, stem cell applications, and what all else we do and don't do with the basic cellular stuff of life. How mega businesses and stock markets operate can affect the fates of governments as well as your and my pension.

The 2000s! It's hard to believe we are already past the halfway mark of the first decade of a new century. With the devastating jolt of 9/11, many of us entered a before and after understanding of our lives and world, something like the before and after divide Pearl Harbor had for generations just before us. In his *The World is Flat*, Thomas Friedman describes the shrinkage of the earth caused by the unrelenting acceleration of communication and transportation.[3] (When I call Dell to order supplies for my home computer, I get a service person in India.) Time will tell if the Iraq War will become as divisive as the Vietnam War. Thus far, though there is disagreement over the wisdom of the war and questions about prisoner treatment and right to privacy, there seems to be a near unanimity of support and appreciation for the service men and women at risk and in harm's way. In early 2006, we are off to a new round of accusations about the integrity of members of Congress relating to unscrupulous influence and money exchanges between leaders and lobbyists. And what will the next decade bring?

Whew! We've come a long way back to the future from Atticus and Scout's front porch.

What's the point? For sure, we face some realities that the people before us did not, as they faced situations unique to their time. Yet there are some ongoing human-spiritual integrity matters that we all face (or ignore at our peril) in our time on the planet.

All along the way, parents teach and live their lives before their children. People decide how and if to keep their promises to one another. Human sexuality is here to stay and we are ever faced with how to steward that gift in a way that builds up and does not tear down. People decide what it means to be a responsible member of the business and political community. We seek the truth and the right thing to do, and even more, we struggle to live that truth and do that right thing once we catch a glimmer of them. In our work and community life, humans continue to explore the interrelationship between our self-interest and compassion for each other. We inevitably fail along the way, and so we seek the ways to be restored and forgiven when we betray our integrity. Underlying the huge quest to determine what integrity requires, there is an even more poignant quest. That is the spiritual quest to find the strength and courage to sustain and live out what integrity requires.

We may not spend as much time in conversation on the porch as Atticus and Scout did in the 1930s. More often now, conversation may be in the car on the way, grabbing a quick burger, or by email. Yet the hunger to live rightly (firm values) and consistently (wholeness), to be people of integrity, continues in us. What follows is an exploration of what being people of integrity means, why it matters, and what makes it possible. Attention to the dearth and rebirth of integrity is a central concern and project for each generation. Now, it is our time.

A Work In Progress Definition

Along the way I have heard different versions of the quip "People's ethics are who they are, what they do, when no one is watching, or when they think no one is watching." This tongue-in-cheek statement might also be connected to "integrity": Who we really are and what we actually do when there is no audience. Yet that goes only so far. Our lives are immersed in relationships. Even what we say and do "when no one is looking" is always connected in some way with our family and friends, colleagues at work and school, life with people in our churches and communities, and beyond.

Here is my perspective for this exploration of integrity: I write as a pastor and preacher. For almost thirty years, my task has been somehow to weave together theological study and reflection with preaching, teaching, leadership, pastoral care, and the wonderful myriad relationships in local church congregations. Being a pastoral theologian, someone has said, means "getting wholesale into retail," an exercise of what John Wesley called "practical divinity." Only a very few persons around a local church want to discuss the finer points of eschatology, hermeneutics, deontological versus teleological ethics, and such. Yet people do want to understand how God is involved with their lives, with the wonderful and awful things that happen, with making hard decisions and dealing with rocky relationships, with hungers and hurts of the planet, and with the mystery of death and beyond.

The 2004 *United Methodist Discipline* says, "Theology is our effort to reflect upon God's gracious action in our lives."[4] People who hang out around churches do want to discover the meaning and presence of God's action in their lives. Pastoral preaching and teaching seek to report what we people together are (and sometimes are not) witnessing and experiencing of God in our lives. In recent years, I have sought to give such voice with what I call bottom lines and working definitions of hard to "wordify" things like grace, joy, love, hope, faith, peace, and . . . integrity.

Though by no means limited to it, the forty day Tithe of Time of Lent that leads up to Easter is a season of faith and life for Christians take a sober, honest look at our lives. We look at our values and actions in relationship to the life, teachings, death, and resurrection of Jesus, the Christ. Each year has its own crop of abuse of power, greed, and lust cases in the news. We struggle in our own set of circumstances and web of relationships. Many of us live with our own personal "9/11 before and afters" with what has and has not happened to us. The prospect-possibility-promise of a life of integrity continues to both haunt us and give us hope.

The Gospel of John begins with powerful words about the Integrity One from God that took on flesh and lived among us full of grace and truth. No shepherds, stars, wise men, manger, or friendly beasts, John's Prologue with magisterial simplicity affirms: "And the Word became flesh and lived among us." The theological word for this mystery is "incarnation"—enfleshment, embodiment, enskinment[5]—of God's love in the flesh and face of Jesus. God's integrity—God's words and actions—aligned in Jesus. This is not proved by an argument or by Bible verses pounded into people. It is authenticated in the experience of countless people through the centuries and around the world— even in the likes of you and me.

Along the way, we will meet some people in integrity formation, to whom John's Gospel introduces us: Nicodemus, the Samaritan woman at the well, the blind man, and at the center of them and us all: Jesus. With a lot of help, here's my working definition of integrity.

> Integrity is the God given strength to respond to life in relation-
> ship to God, instead of reacting to things on our own.

This does not take away from the idea of integrity as acting from firm values and an aligned wholeness in one's life. In a measure, Atticus incarnated his values in the way he did his work and raised his children. He had integrity because his words and actions were in alignment. His lawyer part of life and father part of life were congruent, consistent, and whole. This working definition, however, recognizes that such a life is not something we figure out, set our mind to, grit our teeth, and pull off totally on our own. No one can live such a life for us, but not a one of us can embody such a life on our own. The wisdom to figure out and the strength to live out come from that gracious One who gives us life in the first place.

If you were to suggest that "faith" or "love" or, even better, "being a disciple of Jesus" can easily be interchanged with the word "integrity," you will not get an argument from me. Yet this so-called working definition of "integrity" has continued to work on me and I on it in recent years. These chapters are investments in that ongoing exploration of the grounds and meaning of a life of integrity and Christian faith.

This working definition is, in turn, an outgrowth of another even more fundamental bottom line working definition that has emerged in my ministry and life. A few years ago, I attempted to hone a sentence for which my now thirty-plus years worth of more than 1,000 sermons, myriad articles, and teaching notes would be "footnotes." Here it is:

> God's grace in Jesus Christ gives us the pattern and power to live
> with joy, serve with love, and die with hope.

The "pattern" by which to "respond instead of react" will be explored in chapter 2. In this, we will see how those "firm values" of integrity are discerned. The "God given strength and power," namely "grace," to respond instead of react will be the discussed in Chapter 3. Here, we will look for the spiritual center needed for the wholeness and consistency of integrity. Additional chapters explore various facets of integrity, which will help us move toward a clearer understanding of our call to serve God with integrity in our work and our relationships with people in our family, church, community, and world.

I close this chapter with those people who hang out around churches in my mind and heart. I have spent my life hanging out with them. Church people are not necessarily better or worse than anyone else. Sometimes, by grace, they do soar above the crowd. On occasion, they can be worse, because, by grace, they/we ought to know and do better than the crowd. All in all, the huge majority of church people, like most people, are faithful in their relationships. They seek to be good parents and friends. They do their work competently. Within their means, they are generous with their giving. They try to tell the truth and treat people fairly. They seek—always by grace—to live as forgiven and forgiving people, to face their hardships with courage, their lives with joy, and their deaths with hope.

What's more, they live with such integrity often before the backdrop of those high profile famous and infamous leaders and celebrities who don't. They live with such integrity in a post 9/11 world churning with environmental, financial, and terrorist-military uncertainty. While some might ask, "What's the use?", they just do it. I believe people of such bottom line integrity do make a difference: for one another, for the communities in which live, and to the God of Jesus Christ. They are God's seed, God's kingdom growing people.

Reflections for Spiritual Formation

Reflection One

Any relationship is built on honesty between two beings. Integrity in a relationship means being our true selves, even before God. In Matthew 6:1-8, Jesus instructs us on how to pray with integrity: Pray sincerely and from the heart.

Set up a prayer "closet" or a special quiet or sacred space to pray and study Scripture. This may include a comfortable chair with good lighting, a small table to hold your Bible and a journal and a cup of tea or other beverage. Gather pencils, pens, highlighters, and anything else you might need. Establish a time each day—even as little as 10 minutes—to spend with God in your sacred space.

_____

_____

_____

_____

How might a "sacred space" help you in your relationship of integrity with God? Write your answer in the space provided or in a journal.

Prayer One

Breath prayers are wonderful ways to "pray without ceasing," as Paul says in 1 Thessalonians 5:17. You can pray breath prayers anywhere, at any time. Just pray silently the first part of the prayer as you slowly inhale, and then pray the rest of the prayer on the exhale.

For today, use this verse from the Beatitudes as a breath prayer to focus your day:

Blessed are the merciful, for they shall receive mercy.

Reflection Two

Read Mathew 7:24-27 quickly.

Now, read it again slowly, savoring each word. Imagine someone building a house on a firm foundation. Now imagine someone building a house on the beach.

Tsunamis, hurricanes, floods, and mudslides—we can easily envision houses built on foundations that are not firm. What is God saying to you in this passage of Scripture about personal integrity? How firm is your foundation? How do you establish and maintain a relationship to God? Write your answers in the space provided in the margins or in a journal.

Prayer Two

O God, one hymn proclaims that the firmest foundation of all is "your excellent Word."[6] We give you thanks that our footing is on such solid ground. In the name of the mighty Word we pray. Amen.

Reflection Three

Matthew 5–7 offers an understanding of prayer as the foundation for establishing a relationship with God in order to create a response of integrity. This is especially true in Matthew 6:7-14. Throughout these chapters, Jesus intimates at least three directives for prayer:

> Pray for others in the community to become whole persons ("Beatitudes"), forgive you and others who have hurt them, and be loved.

> Pray for yourself to have courage and strength, forgive others (as you are forgiven), be more loving and more like God.

Write a prayer using these directives.

_____

_____

_____

_____

_____

_____

Prayer Three

Lord, teach me to pray. Amen.

CHAPTER ONE NOTES

1. Harper Lee, *To Kill a Mockingbird*, 86
2. Haynes Johnson, *The Best of Times: The Boom and Bust Years if American Before and After Everything Changed*, p. 144. Original title *The Best of Times: America in the Clinton Years*
3. Thomas L. Friedman, *The World is Flat: A Brief History of the Twenty-first Century*
4. *The United Methodist Book of Discipline 2004*, p. 74
5. "Enskinment": Yes, I know it's not in the dictionary. It's what my friends call a "Morganism": a word I cobble. Such so-called "Morganisms" are hard on English teachers, editors, and my computer spell-check.
6. "How Firm a Foundation," *United Methodist Hymnal*, p. 529

Chapter Two

The Integrity Response

Integrity is the God given strength to *respond* to life in relationship to God, instead of *reacting* to things on our own.

Response vs. Reaction

As a then young associate pastor, fresh from a seminary doctoral project on *Moral Education of Adults in the Church,* I did a several week study with a then young adult class at First UMC, Huntsville, Alabama. (The thens and nows keep stretching out!) We were exploring how a church can be a community of moral discourse, how we assess and make ethical decisions. Among us were people in teaching, engineering, business, law, and medical careers, as well as a number of folks with no bells and whistles. "Just job jobs," one of them put it.

Most were in the first ten or so years of career, marriage, and parenthood. The early rush of those endeavors was beginning to subside and reality was setting in. In various ways, we were discovering that the right thing to do was not always easy to figure out and/or do. Looking back on this, aware of the "accounting scandals" of recent years, I recall a young accountant sharing how he struggled with practices that were technically legal but to his mind were not right.' Others gave examples from their lives and work.

We had extended conversation about the difference between a response and a reaction. People react almost without thought, almost mechanically, at times. On other occasions, we respond, if perhaps for only an instant, by thinking, processing, deciding what to do. Our neurologist in the class explained how reactions and responses come from different parts of the brain. Reactions come from the primal "lower functions" of the brain, areas we share with many animals. Responses, on the other hand, come from the more sophisticated frontal lobe "higher functions" of the brain, levels of cognitive reasoning found pretty much only in humans.

Examples of reactions that get us in trouble are easy to come by. "Fight or flight" are usually given as the two expressions of reactions. Someone hits us; we hit back. Someone says something that makes us mad, and we fire a comeback. Reactions can spiral and escalate. Though these reactions are usually verbal instead of physical, the verbal fight spiral can damage relationships and make problems worse in family, job, and community disputes. On the flight side, we react to physical or verbal assault by backing off in fear or shrinking off in embarrassment, hurt feelings, and resentment. Other forms of reactions can also undermine relationships and communities. Racial, gender, and social class prejudice, stereotyping, and so-called profiling result in reactions to people instead of responding to them.

The neurologist in our class cautioned us against making the reaction capacity of our brains a villain. When perchance we accidentally put our hand on a hot stove, we really don't need to think about and discuss what's cooking. By the grace of our cranial equipment, our synapsial-neural wiring instantaneously swings into action—reacts—and jerks the hand away! In the savannah days of human beings, the fight or flight reaction saved our ancestors' lives. When a wild animal showed up, discourse was not an option. You reflexively, quickly got or got away from the critter before it got you. Driving in the modern day savannahs of traffic, quick reactions—hit the brakes, swerve—can save our lives. Developing good habits can result in a kind of reflexive reactions of kindness, courtesy, and honesty with people.

Having noted that value as well as the danger of reactions in human life, we, nevertheless, recognize that caring, appropriate responses to one another, to our challenges, problems, and opportunities are the way of people of integrity. With one another and ourselves, we have to process what is right, what values are at stake, how what we do is consistent and from a spiritual center.

In the spirit of Wesleyan classes and bands, that group of young adults did become something of a community of moral discourse, not just a place for coffee, doughnuts, and platitude Sunday School lessons. Although at the time we may have referred to our intent as seeking to be mature Christians, we were in other words very much seeking to be people of integrity. We explored together how to be people who respond carefully instead of reacting abruptly with their words and acts. Being people of integrity who respond instead of react touches the whole panoply of our relationships: marriage and family life, projects and disputes with colleagues at work, participation in the larger community with competing causes of various groups, and the not always conflict free life of the church with rival claims for priorities, ministries, and finances.

That considered responses are preferable to knee-jerk reactions in human life is fairly self-evident. Yet it's one of those easier-said-than-done things in life. How do people of integrity go about the formation of appropriate responses? What are the guidelines and goals? The key word here is *discernment*.

The Discernment of Sheep and Life

God's grace in Jesus Christ gives us the *pattern* and power to live . . .

Our word "discern" comes from the Latin words *cernere* and *discernere* meaning "to separate," 'to distinguish." Somewhere along the way, I got the notion that the word was related to the shearing of a sheep; the actual flesh and blood critter looks considerably different once the fluff is shorn away. My dictionary indicates that the Latin word *discernere* expresses "to sift," suggesting the image of sifting wheat, securing the useable grain from the chaff.

People of integrity seek to discern with intellectual honesty, emotional maturity, moral clarity, and spiritual centeredness how to understand what is at stake in their lives and how to speak and act accordingly. First John 4:1 touches on this. "Beloved, do not believe every spirit, but test the spirits to see whether they are from God . . . ." For people of Christian faith, what we know about God and life is tested, sifted, and shorn by the pattern for living we find in Jesus the Christ. This pattern enables us to discern our circumstances and shape our responses.

Noticing how many WWJD? (What would Jesus do?) wristbands, tee shirts, key chains, and such that were around in recent years, a colleague playfully quipped, "Do you know what was on Jesus' wristband when he was growing up?" When I said I didn't know, he smiled and replied, "Why, WWMD?, of course. What would Moses do?"

What would Jesus do? That is such a disarmingly simple, direct way to get at the heart of how we discern what is at stake in our lives, shape our responses, make our decisions, speak and act in our predicaments and situations. It is reminiscent of the classic little book *In His Steps* written by Charles M. Sheldon over a century ago.⚹ A group of people in a church in a small town commits together to make all their decisions for the next year solely based on their understanding of what Jesus would do.

A case can be made that the WWJD? approach is a bit simplistic and naive, that the theme of *In His Steps* is at best quaint in our twenty-first-century, high-tech, low-touch, fast track world. Jesus lived in a totally different era than we do. I was in a playful, but serious, discussion not long ago with a group that got into it over the question, "What kind of car would Jesus drive?" Would it be a sleek presidential limousine, a protective Pope-mobile, or would it be a tin can jalopy befitting the Messiah who came not to be served but to serve? The edgy question that actually emerged was, "How much luxury should Christians allow themselves in a hungry world?" hmm?.

Most all of what Jesus taught about how to speak, act, and live is based on those commandments associated with Moses. Jesus summed up what is at stake in life with the commandments to love God with our all and to love others as we love ourselves. He gets our attention with the parable of the last judgment in Matthew 25, "How you treat the least person is the same as treating me that way." Yet even if we do acknowledge that we are to love our enemies, what does that mean? That doesn't tell me exactly what to do with my "enemy" trying to get the promotion I want or about the terrorist leader half way around the world. Life can be considerably more complex than an easy, breezy "just do what Jesus would do" motto.

So, with due caution about being simplistic and trite, I still find that the WWJD? approach connects and communicates with a wide variety of people about the pattern and model Jesus gives us for discerning what is at stake with our decisions and actions in our life situations. Though the approach may have its limits in the world of academic, "wholesale" theological ethics, it can be an effective tool in the world of everyday, "retail" practical theology. Though the approach does not exempt us from discerning the concrete words and actions to be expressed in actual situations, it points us to the One who gives us the pattern, model, and stories by which to fashion our responses.

Walter Wink is a New Testament scholar who bridges the wholesale and retail worlds of theological reflection and application. In the 1980s, Wink worked with clergy and laypeople in South Africa in their efforts to overcome the cruel racial segregation and economic deprivation of apartheid. He used his study of Jesus' Sermon on the Mount to delineate what he calls "Jesus' Third Way." Wink reminds us that our WWJD? approach depends on a prior question: WDJD? or, "What did Jesus do?"

What Jesus did, according to Wink, was to open people to a new way of living and responding beyond our two primal reaction responses: fight or flight. Wink's study of Matthew 5:38-41 reveals this "third way." Jesus replaces the pattern of eye for eye vengeance with the pattern of non-violent resistance to evil, of turning the cheek, of giving your shirt also if asked for your coat, of going the second mile. Take away the religious sentimentality that has been attached to these verses over the years and we have what some might call an ethic for wimps, a glorified version of "flight." Run away, give in, be passive, be a doormat when people treat you badly. Not so. Jesus presents a creative, courageous response in to replace an anemic reaction.

Wink contends the correct translation is not "do not resist one who is evil" but "do not retaliate with violence." He then looks at the "when you are hit on the right cheek, turn the other cheek" passage. In a right-handed world, a right-handed person would likely strike a person on the right not with a fist but with a backhand. Wink realized Jesus was talking about a master with a servant or an occupying force Roman soldier with a citizen, that is, a situation of unequal power. When one in power strikes an underling, the usual reaction is some form of flight: run away or give in. The fight reaction would only escalate the violence upon the one with less power. Jesus counsels a third alternative. Don't cower away (flight) or slug back (fight); simply stand there, forcing the master to deal with you as a person not a thing. This can also cause the master to look at himself in a new light. A similar dynamic goes on in the cloak and second mile situations.[2]

Rosa Parks essentially responded with the third way of Jesus when she refused to give up her seat on the Montgomery bus in 1955. She moved beyond flight and fight. She didn't move from her seat, and she did not retaliate to the verbal attack of the driver. Her third way played a part in the transformation of our society. Her non-violent resistance was not a flight or fight reaction but a courageous, creative response. Such creative, non-violent resistance, responses played a huge part in the end of apartheid in South Africa. Wink notes that even the black charwomen who had the courage to simply call their white ladies of the house by their first name played a part.[3]

What does this mean for living in our families, for dealing with the situations at work, in the community, and in the church? What does this mean in a 9/11 world as we deal with the market-financial roller coaster, terrorist threats, issues that polarize us like sexuality and abortion? What Did Jesus Do? What Would Jesus Do? Seldom are there quick answers. But Jesus does give us the pattern and a model. It involves finding a third way of creative response. It includes people that others exclude. It involves ongoing forgiveness, going multiple second miles, and giving multiple chances. In order to discern what is at stake and to shape a response, people of integrity pray, engage in Bible study, research the issues involved, partner with others in dialogue and effort, "try stuff," in the search for a creative response. Such "stuff" to be tried often involves hands-on service, face-to-face occasions to know people dealing with poor housing, working without a livable wage, or enduring incarceration.

When people in churches seek to be people of integrity by thinking globally and by acting locally, creative responses emerge. The large number of church people and other community volunteers who participate in Habitat for

Humanity housing projects help meet some of the housing needs for low-income persons. In those efforts they often find a connection with others with whom they may otherwise disagree politically or theologically. They often find a connection with the recipients with whom they likely have a lot more in common than expected.

Concerned about the effort to transition single mothers from welfare to work, a group in a local church studied the issues. They found that, beyond getting a job, there are childcare needs, transportation needs, and an array of work readiness, training, and ongoing encouragement matters. Some thirty people formed into three groups of ten, with each group partnered with a single parent family. They sought to give encouragement and to network in the community on behalf of these families and others for job development, childcare, and transportation options.

Habitat falls far short of meeting all housing needs. The "welfare to work" initiative of that local church was quite limited in its impact. Yet in terms of the often used story of the starfish thrower, on a seashore of washed ashore starfish, with too many for anyone to throw all of them back into the water, what is done does make a difference for the ones thrown back in, as well as for the thrower.

God Beyond and In it All

> Integrity is the God given strength to respond to life *in relationship to God* instead of reacting to things on our own.

A few years back, before subsequent controversy surrounding him, Mel Gibson was in the movie *Signs*. He plays Graham Hess, a minister who has lost his faith because of the seemingly random, senseless accidental death of his wife. In the way movies can make the unbelievable believable, *Signs* is a story about how unfriendly visitors from outer space show up and for a while threaten the earth in general and Graham's family—his two young children, his brother who lives with them, and himself—in particular.

In one scene, Graham, the kids, and brother Merrill are cowering on the couch together as they watch disturbing TV news reports. Merrill asks

Graham, his troubled minister brother, for assurance. Graham says words to the effect that there are two kinds of people. The first group are those who believe in miracles. They believe that there are reasons why things happen and that there is a higher power—God—above and within it all that holds things and us together. The second group believes that things just happen, there's no God to help, and we just have to go it alone, doing the best we can in bad situations. Though Graham is persuasive on behalf of the first way, to Merrill's dismay, Graham confesses he is now in the second group.[4]

The story really is not so much about invaders from outer space as it is an exploration of the inner space of our human faith and the inter-space of caring relationships in a wonderful but an exceedingly dangerous, unpredictable world. The film depicts Graham's eventual journey back to group one.

People of integrity, using the pattern for living provided by Jesus the Christ, seek to respond to life *in relation to God* instead of reacting to things on their own. Yet this "God beyond and in it all" is not always apparent. Bad things indeed happen to good people. So much more about that can be said. But for now, I want to be clear that I am aware that just as the WWJD? pattern is easier talked about than lived out, I am aware that God's presence, even existence, cannot always be taken for granted by many of us. Yet I believe that the greatest expressions of integrity often happen not only in spite of but perhaps because of sojourns into Graham's Group Two. Integrity is living our marriage vows on the days that we don't want to be married, showing tender-tough love with our kids in times when we don't feel very parental, and being God's moral-faithful people with our work even on the days we have more doubts than usual.

In my seminary and graduate training, the theologian and ethicist (theology, what we believe, and ethics, how we live because of what we believe) on whom I concentrated was H. Richard Niebuhr. Niebuhr was pretty much a "wholesale," academic thinker about matters of the nature of God, of how Jesus enables humans to live moral lives, of what it means to be persons and the church in the world. With his study, teaching, and writing, he was actively engaged in understanding and responding to the great issues of war and peace, racism, economic justice, Jesus and the moral life, moral discernment and action. Still, he never became a household name or wrote snappy 1-2-3 how to live your life books. Across my years as a preacher, teacher, writer, and pastor, I seldom mention or quote him. Yet his insights about God, faith, moral living, facing life and death are in the background of most all I say and do in my practical theology "retail" work as a pastor . . . as well as in my own pilgrimage as a person of faith.

Niebuhr developed a concept called "radical monotheism." In a multi-layered way, he drew out the case for and meaning of belief in one beyond-it-all and in-it-all God. One can see the links to Niebuhr's radical monotheism with the first commandment to have no gods but God and Jesus' Great Commandment to love God with our all. Niebuhr, like Martin Luther and others, portrayed how we humans have many operational little gods. Though we might not call them god, by the way that we use them to give our lives meaning, they function that way. Such things as self, family, race, social class, religious denomination, a particular cause, money, or nation can become gods, doing damage not so much by what good they include, but by what good their limited loyalties exclude.[5]

Our culture rightly places great value on families. As spouses, parents, children, siblings, and extended family, we seek to care for, be faithful to, and even sacrifice for one another in our families. In the words of Robert Frost , "Home is the place where, when you have to go there, They have to take you in."[6] Much comment and debate are exerted about the "breakdown of the family" and "family values" in our society. Our family and families need great care and commitment. Yet the good of family love and loyalty becomes something of an idol, something destructive, when my great devotion to my family stops with my family. Family, sadly, can wind up being selfishness multiplied by the three or four who live in our household. In a like manner, the healthy pride and love for ourselves, our ethnic heritage, or nation become destructive idols when we let those loyalties pretty much write off those beyond our group.

Niebuhr spoke of the great life giving and saving God encountered in the Bible and the Christ—the source-force of whom we find hints in the fierce beauty of nature, in human conscience, in the intricacy of cells and complexity of space—as "this One beyond all the many, this power present in all the powers, this reason present in all reasons, this idea inclusive of all ideas, this nature behind and through all natures, this environment environing all of our environments."[7] This universal God does not eliminate our important loyalties and faithfulness to valuable persons, groups, and causes. This God, beyond it and in it all, conditions and transforms our loyalties and relationships. I do not stop loving and serving my family, but the universal God of all families stretches me to care beyond my own family circle, to guard against family love becoming multiplied-disguised selfishness.

People of integrity do not stop caring about their families, group, neighborhood, or country. But the God beyond all the gods causes us to respond with sensitivity and care for those beyond as well as in our immediate circle. We serve God by seeking to serve God in and through the people and situations at hand in our lives. Says Niebuhr: "Responsibility affirms: 'God is acting in all actions upon you. So respond to all actions upon you as to respond to his action'"[8] Those words are evocative of Jesus in Matthew 25, "whatever you do to the least person, you do to me."

About the presence and pattern of God in Christ for our discernment, Niebuhr says:

> For us who are Christians, the possibility of making this new interpretation of the total action of the One who embraces and is present in the many is inseparably connected with an action in the past that was the response of trust by a man who was sent into life and sent into death and to whom answer was made in his resurrection from the dead. Of that resurrection we may know no more than that he lives and is powerful over us and among us.[9]

Niebuhr's words bring to mind Paul's words to the great intellects of Athens in Acts 17, concerning God as "the one in whom we live and move and have our being." In one of his sermons on The Sermon on the Mount, John Wesley, founder of the Methodist movement, said about the mystery of God's presence in the persons and events of our lives:

> God is in all things . . . we are to see the Creator in the glass

36

(window) of every creature . . . we should use and look upon nothing as separate from God, which indeed is a kind of practical atheism; but with a true magnificence of thought survey heaven and earth and all therein as contained by God in the hollow of his hand, who by his intimate presence holds them all in being . . . and is in a true sense the soul of the universe.[10]

Dearth: A scarcity that makes more dear. A dearth and rebirth of integrity. Atticus the lawyer seeks to act with integrity so he can hold his head up before his children in a world that often jeers more than cheers such moral courage. Graham the minister seeks a sign that God is in the world after all, a world whose horrors and hurts can cause us to wonder where and if God is. People of integrity seek to respond instead of reacting. They seek to discern how the pattern of Jesus assesses their predicaments and shapes their responses. And they seek to find hints of the universal God in the messy particulars of their lives.

Amazingly, at times, we may pretty well know what integrity calls for. Yet finding the strength to actually speak and act with that integrity can feel like trying to pick up ourselves by our shoe strings or by the short hairs of our necks. To have the pattern by which to live with integrity, but not to have the power and stamina to pull off the pattern is an exquisite torture. The good news, however, is that at the heart of things is not a giant threatening demand for us to straighten up and live right or else. At the heart of it all, there is a great grace that empowers us to live with integrity, to be and do what we could never accomplish on our own. To this power, we now turn.

Reflections for Spiritual Formation

Reflection One

Dr. Morgan speaks of Jesus as the pattern by which we discern "with intellectual honesty, emotional maturity, moral clarity and spiritual centeredness how to understand what is at stake in (our) lives and act accordingly." However, the reality is that even with all that, sometimes our decisions do not have good outcomes or have an outcome we did not expect.

Reflect quietly on a recent decision you made that did not turn out the way you thought it might, even though you carefully and prayerfully did all you could to discern rightly. Are you able to let the decision go and to move on? In other words, is your relationship with God such that you can trust that "all things work together for good for those who love God, who are called according to His purpose"? (Romans 8:28) Write your response in the space provided.

_____

_____

_____

_____

_____

_____

Prayer

Theologian Reinhold Niebuhr is credited with writing the following prayer that has been adopted by Alcoholics Anonymous. As you pray it throughout the day today, "chew on" the words, savoring their meaning, particularly as it relates to serenity, courage, and wisdom.

The Serenity Prayer

God, grant me the serenity to accept the things I cannot change,
The courage to change the things I can,
And the wisdom to know the difference.
Amen.

Reflection Two

Acts 17:1-15 illustrates two differing viewpoints after much discernment from the parties involved. In both cases, Paul offered Scripture as a way of discerning the truth about Jesus Christ. Could it be that the people in Thessalonica had as one of their "operational little gods" their status and role in the synagogue and community? Why do you think the people in Beroea "got it" while the people in Thessalonica did not? What are some of your "operational little gods"? When have they gotten in the way of your discernment to do the right thing? Write your answers in the space provided or in your journal.

_____

_____

_____

_____

_____

_____

_____

_____

Write a prayer about this.

_____

_____

_____

_____

_____

_____

_____

_____

_____

_____

Prayer

"I am the Lord, your God, who brought you out of the land of Egypt, out of the house of slavery. You shall have no other gods before me. (Exodus 20:2-3)

"Hear, O Israel, the Lord is our God, the Lord alone. You shall love the Lord your God with all your heart, and with all your soul, and with all your might." (Deuteronomy 6:4-5)

Life-Giving God, we have never worshipped a tree or rock or statue. But sometimes we do make idols of things. At times, we make our pride or anger or need for recognition the center of our lives. Without your care, we can make good things like our loved ones or our job the center of our lives, cutting us off from other people and matters in your world. God, help us recognize your presence in all we do. God, help us love you through the ways we treat people and take care of your world. Amen.

A Retreat with Desert Mystics,
St. Anthony Messenger Press, p. 57.

Reflection Three

In Acts 17:16-21, the Athenians' "operational little god" seems to be their intellectualism—they spent "their time in nothing but telling or hearing something new." What was Paul's argument to them (verses 22-31)? How did they react to Paul's message? Why would Dionysius and Damaris come to believe and follow Paul? How does our intellectualism get in the way of our discernment? How does our intellectualism contribute to our discernment? Is there a Scripture passage that has been helpful to you in making decisions? If so, write it down in the space provided or in your journal. If not, find one now and write it down.

_____

_____

_____

_____

_____

_____

Prayer

For the next twenty-four hours, pray this breath prayer:

God of my mind, illumine me.

CHAPTER TWO NOTES

1. Charles M. Sheldon, *In His Steps*, see bibliography
2. Walter Wink, *Violence and Non-Violence in South Africa: Jesus' Third Way*, pp. 13, 15, 16
3. Wink, p. 22
4. *Signs*, from chapter 10 of the DVD, "Fourteen Lights"

5. H. Richard Niebuhr develops his penetrating concept of 'radical monotheism' in his *Radical Monotheism and Western Culture*; see bibliography.
6. Robert Frost, "Death of the Hired Hand," quoted in *Bartlett's Familiar Quotations*, 15th Edition, (Boston: Little Brown and Company, 1980) p. 747
7. H. Richard Niebuhr, *The Responsible Self*, p. 175
8. Niebuhr, *TRS*, p. 126
9. Niebuhr, *TRS*, p. 143
10. John Wesley, *The Works of John Wesley*, vol. 1, pp. 516f.

Chapter Three

Grace-Fueled Integrity

Integrity is the *God given strength* to respond to life in relationship to God, instead of reacting to things on our own.

God's Grace in Jesus Christ gives us the pattern and *power* to live...

The Gospel According to "Get To"

When we were little boys, my cousin Jimmy liked to rub it in that he is two whole months and four days older than me. That's not a problem for me now! But then it irritated me. We were always competing over things like who could count the highest, run the fastest, spit seeds the farthest. More than once we wound up in a human knot of knees and elbows, red-faced, trying desperately not to be the one who cried or gave up first. One day, when we were five or so, we were playing in our grandparents' yard. Though we did come to an amicable agreement that we wanted some ice-cream, of which Granny's freezer always seemed full, we quickly decided that we had to race to the house to see who could get there first.

We were neck to neck as we neared the house. Just then, Jimmy stiff-armed me into the hydrangea bushes. By the time I scrambled to my feet and caught up, Jimmy was at the top of the back steps about to open the screen door. I was standing about two steps below Jimmy, which put his bottom in front of my face. He had just shoved me down. I had only a nanosecond to act. So, I took a bite. Jimmy wailed. Granny came running to see who had injured whom this time. She pulled up the leg of Jimmy's shorts to show me where in her words I had "bit a plug out of Jimmy." I suggested some Merthiolate and a bandage, probably because I knew that the medicine would sting.

Granny was upset and mad, which got me crying along with Jimmy. "Boys," she scolded, "we are a family. You have *got to* love each other. Now unless you want me to call your daddies, you have *got to* tell each other that you are sorry, and then you have *got to* give each other a hug!" The last thing Jimmy and I wanted to do was hug. But we had to do it. After all, Granny was large from a five-year-old's vantage point, was scary when angry and known to dispense ice cream when pleased. We grudgingly hugged, got the ice cream, and went back to playing, at least until the next altercation.

Decades later, I still resist being told that I have *got to* do something, perhaps more when I know deep down I ought to. Some people even make the Bible a book of things that we have *got to* do or else, telling us that we have *got to* love God and even people we don't like. Being told that I have *got to* love people I don't like makes me want to do it even less. For some, the church comes across as a big Granny telling people what they ought to and have *got to* do, handing out doses of guilt, shame, and threats when people don't shape up.

Courtly Dr. Albert Outler was a world-renowned theologian and churchman, and an expert on the life and theology of Methodist founder John Wesley. Some years ago, I came across an interview that church historian and commentator Martin Marty had with Albert Outler, not too many years before Outler's death. Marty commented that Dr. Outler was a theologian who preached and asked him what he had learned over forty years of such preaching to Christian people. Outler replied something like this: "That I was short of the mark when I used to preach, You have *got* to love. Almost too late, I learned that the Gospel of grace allows me to say, You *get* to love."[1]

That simple but profound distinction opened doors and turned on lights in me. Consider the difference between living life as a *got to* and a *get to*. Instead of groaning, "Oh, God it's morning, I've got to crawl out of bed and go at it again!" it's more like a contented sigh, "Oh, God, I get to have another day of life!" Instead of, "I've got to go to work," it is, "Thank God, I get to have some work to do." Instead of, "I've got to put up with those people again," it's "Thank you, God, I get to have some people to love and to love me." Though it may seldom be quite that simple, and our lives have their shares of *got to*'s that no sugar-coating can disguise, the drag of living life as a *got to* is clearly trumped by living our life as a *get to.*

Such a distinction teaches us that the gospel is grace-fueled not law-driven—not finally a matter of what God demands from us, but what God makes possible for us. Loving God with all our hearts and loving each other as much as we love ourselves are not so much chores God inflicts upon us, but blessings that God enables and empowers us to do. Being people of integrity is not what by God's demand we have *got to* do but what with God's strength and power we *get to* do. Grace takes us from a "duty driven" life to a "joy-empowered" life.

The story of John Wesley's life is frequently told among Methodists. As a young man, Wesley drove himself to be holy in order to be worthy of God's love, forgiveness, and acceptance. He rose early each day to pray and study Scripture. He and his associates worshiped and celebrated communion frequently. He lived frugally and gave generously. He and the other "Methodists" or "Bible moths" at Oxford did jail ministry and worked with the poor. By his own judgment, Wesley never considered it enough. In his early 30s, he went to the British Colony of Georgia to be the priest for the colonists and a missionary to the Indians. Wesley felt if he could help with their salvation then perhaps he could gain his. His religious rigidness with his parishioners and his almost slap-stick failed love relationship with Sophy Hopkey caused him such troubles that he fled the colonies and returned to England in early 1738, his thirty-fifth year. Though Wesley lived in many ways a model life, it was a life based on *got to* duty and drudgery, driven by what he understood was required by God, not what is made possible by God's love.

On the voyage to and from the colonies, Wesley observed the Moravian Christians aboard ship. Even in the midst of a frightening storm, their faith held them steady and calm. Both in Georgia and back in England, John had conversations with Moravian pastors about the assurance and awareness of God's forgiveness and acceptance their people had. Many of us are familiar with Peter Bohler's encouragement to Wesley to preach faith until he had it and then to preach faith because he had it.

Such as this is the usual backdrop given to portray John Wesley's dreary state of mind, heart, and life when he went to a religious meeting at Aldersgate Street on May 24, 1738. About a quarter of nine, while someone was reading Martin Luther's commentary on Paul's letter to the Romans, about how we are saved by faith not works, Wesley reported with these often quoted words: "I felt my heart strangely warmed. I felt I did trust in Christ, Christ alone for salvation; and an assurance was given me that He had taken away my sins, even mine, and saved me from the law of sin and death."

In his *The Presence of God in Christian Life: John Wesley and the Means of Grace*, Henry Knight suggests Wesley's Aldersgate experience apparently caused him to look at the Bible, particularly the New Testament, in a new way. Now, Wesley saw the Bible not as much as God's demands and requirements of us for our salvation but more as God's promises to us about the gift of salvation. On June 4, 1738, just days after Aldersgate, Wesley writes in his Journal: "All these days, I scarce remember to have opened the Testament, but upon some great and precious promise. And I saw more than ever, that the Gospel is in truth but one great promise, from the beginning of it to the end."[2]

As far as the salvation of persons and the shaping of Christian character, Knight observes, "Wesley believes every command of God 'has the force of a promise;' the directive to live according to the character of a Christian is at the same time a promise by God to give one that character."[3]

Call it character; call it integrity. From demand to promise, from reacting to responding, from *got to* to *get to* living, the Christian life of integrity is based on the power and strength God gives us to speak and act in ways we never could achieve on our own.

German New Testament theologian Willi Marxsen, 1919-1993, was a world class scholar who worked for the most part in the "wholesale" world of university study, teaching, and academic oriented publications. In my seminary training and ongoing study as a pastor, I have found his writings stimulating. His last book, *New Testament Foundations for Christian Ethics*, offers background resources for us in the "retail" world of practical theology and living as people of integrity. Marxsen gives deep Biblical background for describing the God of Jesus depicted in Scripture as the one who gives not just commands and requirements but the strength and power to live a faithful life, to pull off the Jesus pattern of responding to the universal God in all our particular predicaments.

Marxsen makes clear that the New Testament is not a seamless garment. The gospels and the letters of Paul have their portraits, or as Marxsen said, even snapshots, of the kind of life followers of Jesus live. There is, however, a predominant trajectory of Christian life: a life that is more enabled by God as a gift than demanded by God as an achievement.

Based on a grammatical metaphor coined by New Testament scholar Rudolf Bultmann more than eighty years ago, Marxsen distinguishes between life, faith, and action based on God's presence as an "imperative" and/or an "indicative." An "imperative" sentence issues an order or command, while an "indicative" sentence states a reality, the way things are. The first demands that something be done; the second declares what already is.

In the early part of his book, Marxsen does an extended exposition of Mark 1:14-15. This passage summarizes Mark's depiction of Jesus' message and the new way of life Jesus brings.

> Jesus came to Galilee, proclaiming the good news of God, and saying, "The time is fulfilled, and the kingdom of God has come near; repent, and believe in the good news."

Often, we jump to the "imperative" command-demand: repent. Do something to be right with God. Repentance comes from the New Testament Greek word *metanoia. Meta* means "beyond," as "going beyond where one is now, change" The *noia* part of the word comes from the Greek word for "knowledge," which we can hear in the first syllable of that English word. *Noia* can also refer to "mind." *Metanoia* can be rendered as "change of mind." That, however, does not do justice to the radical nature of *metanoia*. This is not a mere change of mind: to have a hamburger instead of a taco for lunch, or even to try to do better with our job. *Metanoia* is more like a combination head and heart transplant, the total transformation, reorientation, and redirection of a life.

Marxsen urges us to notice that before that imperative, Mark makes an indicative statement: God's kingdom (Greek: *basileia*) is near. All that the New Testament term "kingdom of God" means and suggests goes way beyond our efforts here. Yet suffice it to say, God's kingdom refers to the mystery of God's presence, God's new reality in which people live in forgiven and forgiving relationship with God and one another. Mark's proclamation, the simple yet profound clarification that Marxsen is making, is that the "indicative" reality of God's timely, near presence makes it possible for us to follow the "imperative"—repent—"to change our lives," perhaps better, "be changed." Often we err by seeming to say we must change/repent before God's forgiveness/acceptance will come, that is, doing something to earn and be worthy of them. In truth, the total "turning around" of our lives is something we cannot do on our own. The "indicative" makes the "imperative" possible.

> By Jesus' actions toward people they experienced the indicative that enabled them to act the way they were invited to by the proclamation.[4]

> Jesus was experienced by his disciples as someone who in his work lived his God for them. And this changed people. For them the love of enemy is not something they are ordered to do by commandment and therefore must do. Love of enemy is something they do because they can.[5]

Marxsen devotes a large portion of his book to the theology/Christology and ensuing ethics of Paul. Here, he explores the "paradox" of the "imperative" and "indicative" in Paul's portrayal of the new way of life that Jesus' life, death, and resurrection makes possible for humanity and the world. "All this," Paul writes to the Corinthians, "is from God, who reconciled us to himself *through* Christ, and has given to us the ministry of reconciliation." (2 Corinthians 5:18, emphasis mine) The first part of the sentence is a clear indicative and the second part, our ministry of reconciliation in the world, communicates an imperative, yet one not demanded but enabled by the indicative. Thus, our actions to live moral, responsible lives of integrity are not efforts exerted *for* God but enabled *by* God.

Our words and acts in service to God and others then become more *gifts* than *tasks*, more *fruit* than *works*. "In Pharisaic ethics, people must always *change their ways* in order to accomplish works. In the Christian Paul's ethic, people must *let themselves be changed*, so they can bear fruit." [6]

Though Marxsen writes with appropriate scholarly reserve, I sensed a sort of quiet joy bubbling up in his words. His exegesis and interpretation of major portions of the New Testament reveals a way of life made possible for humanity by this God who through Christ initiates and empowers responsible living and hopeful dying.

The "Gospel According to 'Get To'" is a playful yet serious phrase. Being people of integrity is not something we have got to do on our own limited energy but is something we get to do by the abundant power and strength God gives us. The conviction that we can be people of integrity who respond instead of react in the situations and predicaments of our lives is based on our experience of a beyond our own doing strength that God gets to us. In a word, we have been talking about grace all along. Yet more needs to be said. What's more, John Wesley's portrayal of grace has few rivals.

> God's *grace* in Jesus Christ gives us the pattern and *power* to live . . .

John Wesley's House of Grace

Over my twenty-five-plus years as a United Methodist pastor, I have come to observe that there are two groups of Methodists.

> Group 1: "I have not always been a Methodist. But I feel very much at home in the Methodist Church. Still, I am not exactly sure what we Methodists believe."

49

Group 2: "I have always been a Methodist. I wouldn't want to be anything else. But I am still not exactly sure what we Methodists believe."

On some occasions, this conversation arises after a church member has taken it on the chin from one of his or her apparently know-exactly-what-they-believe, other denomination, hard-liner friends. Encouraging the assailed member not to argue back or be intimidated, I suggest a smiling one-liner response to that "what do you/we Methodists believe?" query, which is, "Well, there's a lot more to it, but it has a lot to do with grace."

Thanks to DISCIPLE Bible Study groups galore and other such small group studies as *Christian Believer*, Emmaus reunion groups, and such, I do not have this conversation as much as I once did. I am witnessing a greater number of biblically and theologically well-informed and formed people in the church and community. They are getting to know better this amazing grace of God in Christ, especially as it is depicted in the life and thought of John Wesley. People find that Wesley's insights are profoundly grounded in *Scripture*, informed by the rich Christian *tradition* around the world and through the centuries, shaped by sound *reason* and intellectual honesty, and authenticated in the head-heart-hands realm of human *experience*. (a.k.a Wesley's Quadrilateral)

John Wesley is reported to have produced some 5,000 sermons, criss-crossed Britain some 250,000 miles by horseback and carriage preaching, teaching, and organizing over the course of fifty-plus years of ministry. He was author and editor of almost innumerable books, commentaries, tracts, pamphlets covering all the nooks and crannies of faith and life. Yet he succinctly summarizes it all in *A Plain Account of Christian Perfection*: "We ascribe the whole of salvation to the mere grace of God."[7] Being saved by grace, says Wesley in his sermon "The Means of Grace," is "that great foundation of the whole Christian building."[8]

In *The New Creation: John Wesley's Theology for Today*, Emory University theologian Theodore Runyon writes: "the key to all of Wesley's soteriological doctrines is his understanding of God's grace. But what is grace, and how does it function according to his understanding of salvation?" Citing Wesleyan scholar Randy Maddox's view in *Responsible Grace: John Wesley's*

Practical Theology, Runyon notes that, on one hand, Western theologians (Roman Catholic and Protestant) have generally focused on grace as the external forgiving-relationship restoring action of God's love in Christ on behalf of persons. On the other hand, Eastern theologians (Greek Orthodox and others) have tended to depict grace as the internal transforming-renewing action of God's love within persons. For Wesley, both are aspects of God's grace, which "is most fundamentally God's love for humanity made evident in Christ."[9]

Over recent years in my preaching, teaching, and practice of ministry, I have tried to come up with working definitions of core words of Christian life. A working definition of "grace," one I believe is rooted in Scripture and Wesley, is: *Grace is the beyond-our-own-doing love, help, and strength God gives us, without which we cannot be or do anything that matters.* What follows is a brief overview of Wesley's description of the facets of the grace diamond, or, perhaps better, of the architecture of the house of grace in which we "live and move and have our being." (Acts 17:28)

A look at how Wesley depicts the architecture of grace can generate a spirited discussion, exploring where he got his material, who his sources were, and what is original and what is borrowed. By and large, Wesley's genius was his ability to weave together insights, concepts, and doctrines from across the gamut of theologians, biblical themes, Christian experience, and church traditions. A case can be made that Wesley was a bridge between the Roman Catholic and Protestant Churches, as well as between the Western and Eastern Churches. Albert Outler spoke of Wesley as "a clearsighted synthesizer of a rich multifaceted tradition—that very rare sort of eclectic who actually understood the options he had to choose between."[10]

John Wesley portrays God's life-empowering grace as mysterious, indivisible, timeless, and amazing. "But in order of thinking," says Wesley, we can distinguish aspects of grace and a sort of sequence to aid our understanding.[11] To restore the sin-damaged image of God in humanity, there is a tri-part work of grace: prevenient grace, justifying grace, and sanctifying grace. *Prevenient* grace refers to God's grace active all *around* us. *Justifying* grace indicates God's grace acting *for* us. And *sanctifying* grace expresses God's grace active *in* us.

Prevenient Grace

The word "prevenient" indicates something that "comes before," by extension, something that is ever before us, never absent. By prevenient grace, Wesley refers to the presence of God's love-help-strength is at work in our lives before anything we do, before we have the foggiest notion that grace is afoot. Like air, God's grace is unseen but absolutely essential. This grace enables us to respond to and in grace. "The most profound, yet simplest fact is that you cannot have God without God. The name for this initiative from the other side is grace."[12]

Even with what we now know about socialization and the unconscious, Wesley makes a compelling case for conscience, our internal sense of what is right and wrong, as an element of prevenient grace. "No man sins because he has not grace, but because he does not, use the grace he has."[13] Because of God's abounding, surrounding grace, Wesley considers that grace might have saving power, at least in a provisional, partial way in "Mahometans" (Wesley's term for what we now call "Muslims").[14]

In the rush of a conversion-religious experience, persons sometimes discount the worth of everything and everyone before. ("Well, my family and I went to church, but we weren't 'really' Christians. And I'm not sure if my Sunday school teachers and the preacher were 'really' . . . But now that I have accepted Jesus . . .") Yet in the eyes of mature faith, in retrospect, God's subtle, but effective prevenient grace can be seen at work in it all along—preparing, sustaining, and guiding us. People look back on hard times they have somehow gotten through and recognize "that something more than me got me through that."

Justifying Grace

Justifying grace refers to the Protestant-Western-Reformed emphasis on God's pardoning-forgiving-accepting love given *for* us in and through Jesus Christ. The divine relationship restoring comes apart from what we do or do not merit. This converting grace is received by faith, not work; as a gift, not a reward.

We will see that God's grace does not stop with God's gracious external act *for* us in Christ. God's grace in Christ, as we will see, continues with God's gracious transforming love *in* us through the Holy Spirit. Yet Wesley knows that the Lutheran paradox of *"simul justus et simul peccator"* (always saved and sinner at the same time) is for real. Grace is "that free love, that unmerited mercy, by which I, a sinner, through the merits of Christ am now reconciled to God."[15] We ever depend on the pardoning love of God for us in Jesus.

Some have dramatic experiences of this justifying-forgiving-accepting grace of God in Christ. There is a clear "before" and "after" with their conversion, their coming to Christ. Others do not have a "mountaintop" experience and cannot pinpoint a precise time and place God's love and acceptance for them became to them. In retrospect, they become aware of a gradual growing process. Whether from an exact moment or from reflection on the passage of time, we become aware that God's love in our lives is not something we have accomplished but something we have been given, something done *for* us.

Sanctifying Grace

Sanctifying grace refers to the Catholic-mystical-Eastern emphasis on God's transforming-healing-maturing love at work *in* us through the Spirit. Whereas justification is a western church juridical term expressing an *external* change in our status, sanctification is an Eastern Church therapeutic term expressing an *internal* change in our state.[16] Justification is a sort of external spark that ignites the subsequent internal "new birth" sanctification process that causes us to grow and mature in Christ-based love for God and others. "Whereas faith is the mark of justification, love is the mark of sanctification."[17]

In the realm of sanctification, Wesley speaks of Christian holiness, even of "Christian perfection." This is sometimes misunderstood. By this, Wesley means not so much a mistake free perfection, but a growing completeness of intention to live a love-motivated life. For Wesley, Christian perfection is both as simple and profound as "loving God with all our heart," to love our neighbor as we love ourselves, to love others as Jesus loves them, and "to have the mind that was in Christ."[18] "Sanctification," wrote V.H.H. Green, "was the crown of what was perhaps the most original of all Wesley's doctrines, that of Christian Perfection."[19]

In order, prevenient, justifying, and sanctifying grace are what Wesley calls the Porch, the Door, and House/Rooms of the salvation process.[20] On the porch of our life, God's prevenient grace is ever present. The forgiving-justifying grace of God in Christ is the entrance of a new relationship with God in our lives. And the sanctifying love of God in Christ begins an ongoing rebuilding of the house of our lives, a room by room extended process aiming at every nook and cranny of our being: tongue, wallet, heart, passions, mind, prejudices, values, etc. In a sense, each of us is character-integrity formation work in process building project of God's life-fueling grace.

"To say Christian life depends upon the grace of God is not enough," writes Wesley scholar Henry Knight. "Wesley insisted God's grace was normally mediated through means of grace."[21] Wesley defines "means of grace" as "outward signs, words, or actions ordained by God to ordinary channels whereby God might convey to men preventing, justifying, and sanctifying grace."[22]

One distinction Wesley makes in the means of grace is between *Acts of Piety* and *Acts of Mercy*. Generally, acts of piety refer to our relationship with God and acts of mercy refer to our relationship with one another. Acts of piety include worship, prayer, Bible study, Holy Communion, fasting, Christian conferencing (i.e., holy conversation with others about our relationship to God). In general, Wesley cites works of mercy as *doing no harm and doing good*. Particularities include: feeding the hungry, caring for the sick, housing the homeless, and caring for those at risk in the world.

These activities are not works of righteousness and are not themselves grace. But these practices are (1) the channels by which God's grace comes into our lives, empowering us to live with faithfulness and integrity, and (2) the ways in which we respond to God's grace. Grace-empowered faith needs grace-empowered faithfulness.

Wesley portrays a *spiritual respiration*. We cannot live without the gift-grace of air, but we must respond to it by inhaling and exhaling it. "God's breathing into the soul, and the soul's breathing back what it receives from God; a continual action of God upon the soul; the reaction of the soul upon God . . . all the works of our hands, all our body, soul, and spirit, to be a holy sacrifice." After quoting those words from Wesley's "The Great Privilege of

Being Born of God," Theodore Runyon continues: "To this we are called . . . to take into ourselves continuously that breath of life . . . from the Spirit of God, and continuously to breathe out this same spirit in . . . service to God, our fellow human beings, and all creation."[23]

Henry Knight explores the amazing subtleties and interconnections among the means of grace. Such means of grace as prayer and Bible study can overcome despair with hope, complacency with active love, and presumption with humility. Experience of God's love in worship can lead us to a more disciplined life when we have grown sloppy in our faith and life, or it can free us up for more joyful life when we have become overly demanding of others and ourselves. Holy Communion can have a prevenient grace function, awakening persons to God's love all around them. It can be a justifying experience by which a person comes to faith. And it certainly has an ongoing sanctifying power that helps people to grow in their faith, love, and integrity, to be more aware of their blessings, and to persevere in distress and evil. Wesley never suggests that we can fully understand the mysterious efficacy of the means of grace, only that we practice them.

Means of grace are inextricably related to *communities of grace*—including those people who hang out around churches mentioned earlier. It is said that Wesley's contemporary George Whitefield was a far more scintillating preacher who drew larger crowds than Wesley, that Whitefield could bring tears by the sonorous way he pronounced "Mesopotamia.". Yet no ongoing people or movement resulted from Whitefield's efforts. Why? Methodism was multiplied and sustained by the small groups, the classes and bands, that Wesley and his helpers organized and for which they mentored laity leaders.

The twelve-member classes proved to be superb means of grace. They met weekly for prayer, Bible study, honest sharing of the condition of their lives and souls, and holding one another accountable. Neither rival nor substitute for the larger church, the class meetings helped people experience their faith more up close and personal. They were means of what has been called *accountable discipleship.* Not only did the small groups provide care for one another, they reached out in care and service to others. In recent years, a new vitality is being experienced in many churches through small groups, such as DISCIPLE Bible

Studies, and volunteer groups like Habitat for Humanity Houses or short-term mission trips. The rediscovery of the means of grace of small groups is unleashing new waves of life-changing, integrity-forming grace in people's lives.

In his novel *What's Bred in the Bone,* Robertson Davies tells the story of Francis Cornish. Francis, a Canadian, is traveling in Germany a few years before World War II. He stays as a guest for a while in a huge, old, manorhouse castle. Ruth, a woman also staying at the manorhouse, and Francis get into a deep conversation one day about how humans find their way in life.

They recall the great religious and political struggles that occurred around them in Europe through history, how people are still susceptible to superstition like astrology, even though they claim in the twentieth century to depend upon science. As they talk, it is cold outside yet comfortable inside, their room warmed by a great porcelain stove, a stove with no apparent opening into which to put the firewood. Now conscious of their feeling warm and snug, Ruth asks Francis if he has ever thought about how the stoves in the castle are fed. Come to think of it, he has wondered, but doesn't know how. Ruth explains:

> "That's one of the interesting things about these old castles. Dividing all the main rooms are terribly narrow passages—not more than eighteen inches wide and dark as night and through these corridors creep servants in soft slippers who poke firewood into these stoves from the back. Unseen by us, and usually unheard. We don't give them a thought, but they are there, and they keep life in winter from being intolerable . . . . They keep us warm, they are necessary to us . . . . They are the hidden life of the house."

> "A spooky idea, " Francis replies.

> "The whole universe is a spooky idea," Ruth continues, "and in every life there are these unseen people and—not people exactly—who keep us warm."[24]

Though the world at times can be a house of horrors, Davies in his way, like John Wesley in his way, affirms that it is more a house of grace sustaining us with *beyond-our-own-doing love, help, and strength without which we cannot be or do much that matters.* The longer we live, we come to realize how many people and circumstances along the way carried us along. Yet to connect with that great unseen presence that enlivens every moment, take your next breath or feel your heart beat. Spooky? Perhaps. Sacred? Ah, yes.

To be people of integrity in this world is no small task. Even as we chisel out a course of action that is of moral worth and responsible for what and whom are at stake in our lives, the strength and power to actualize and sustain that course is beyond our capacity. We may bristle when we are told we have "got to" or "ought to" do something. In truth, that resistance often masks our fear that we cannot pull it off or sustain it. There is, then, thank God, the mystery of the unseen grace of God that "keeps us warm," that fuels our lives.

By grace, Atticus Finch in *To Kill a Mockingbird* has the integrity to champion an unpopular and dangerous, yet just, cause. Graham Hess in *Signs* can begin to see again the presence of the One who holds life and us together, and with integrity re-enter his ministry of witnessing to such grace to his people. Such "get to" grace even makes people like my cousin Jimmy and me want to hug each other.

Reflections for Spiritual Formation

Reflection One

Read Mark 1:14-15. What does the kingdom of God look like or mean to you? Where do you see God's kingdom in your life? Do these insights into the kingdom of God make it easier or harder for you to repent? Why or why not? Write your responses in the space provided.

_____

_____

_____

_____

_____

_____

The author points to God's indicative in this passage as the fact that the kingdom of God is near or at hand. In other words, the kingdom of God is around us now, in the present tense. Then the author points out God's imperative: Repent, turn your life around. The second imperative in this passage is to "believe in the good news." Often we forget this second imperative, which may make it harder to do the first one! We need to believe and trust in God's grace to forgive and reconcile us to God in order to venture into the repentance part.

Prayer

Pray this breath prayer for the next twenty-four hours:

God of surprises, let me see you.

Reflection Two

Read 2 Corinthians 5:18-19. Paul says that God *reconciled* God's self to us through Christ. And then God gave us that same power. In other words, we can reconcile ourselves to others or others to ourselves, or even others to others, as in the case of mediation or peace-keeping.

Webster's Dictionary defines reconcile as "to make something consistent or compatible, to bring into harmony." (Think of your checkbook and how you *reconcile* your checkbook at the end of the month: You bring it into harmony with the amount of money you have in your account.) Look at your checkbook or at your latest bank statement. Does it reconcile with a life lived in response to a relationship with God? What do you spend your money on?

In chapter 1, Reflection 2, you were asked to write a prayer using directives from Jesus. Using these same directives, write a prayer directing your efforts at using your money to bring you to reconciliation to God and to others.

_____

_____

_____

_____

_____

_____

Prayer

Read the 23rd Psalm in your favorite Bible version.

After you do this, just look at the verses.

Name some of the ways God has meet your needs . . . home . . . friends . . . another day . . . _____ (fill in your own blank.)

During the day, quietly to yourself, repeat this words as a breath prayer:

"Thank you, God, for all good things that come from you. Amen."

Add this line to the verses above and say them together as a prayer:

"Thank you, God, for all good things that come from you. Amen."

Reflection Three

In 2 Corinthians 5:19, Paul adds to verse 18, saying that not only does God give us the ministry of reconciliation, God *entrusts* it to us. What does this mean to you? God entrusts us with this ministry because God does "not count their trespasses against them." What is your response to this? Are there any "trespasses" of others that you may not have forgiven? How might this prevent you from being a minister of reconciliation? Can you ask God to help you forgive these people as God has forgiven you? And then can you forgive yourself?

The Prayer of Jesus
Our Father who art in heaven,
Hallowed be Thy name.
Thy kingdom come, thy will be done
on earth as it is in heaven.
Give us this day our daily bread.
And forgive us our trespasses
as we forgive those who trespass against us.
And lead us not into temptation,
but deliver us from evil.
For thine is the kingdom,
and the power,
and the glory
forever.
Amen.

CHAPTER THREE NOTES

1. This simple-profound statement of Albert Outler has become a key insight for my understanding of Christian faith and life. I have long lost the printed source. When I wrote Martin Marty about it, he responded, "I still get 'aha's' when I think of the distinction. I'm sure he'd be pleased if you'd use it." Email to author 10/16/02
2. Henry H. Knight III, *The Presence of God in the Christian Life: John Wesley and the Means of Grace*, p. 154
3. Knight, p. 154
4. Willi Marxsen, *New Testament Foundations for Christian Ethics*, p. 41
5. Marxsen, pp. 105f.
6. Marxsen, p. 167

7. John Wesley, *A Plain Account of Christian Perfection*, p. 15
8. John Wesley, *The Works of John Wesley*, vol. 1, p. 383
9. Theodore Runyon, *The New Creation: John Wesley's Theology for Today*, p. 26
10. Quoted in Lovett Weems, *Leadership in the Wesleyan Spirit*, p. 89
11. John Wesley, *John Wesley's Forty-Four Sermons*, "The New Birth," p. 514
12. Runyon, p. 23
13. John Wesley, *The Works of John Wesley*, vol. 3, p. 207
14. Runyon, p. 33
15. Runyon, p. 43
16. Randy Maddox p. 256, Runyon p. 26
17. Runyon, p. 85
18. Wesley, *Plain Account of Christian Perfection*, pp. 29, 30.
19. V. H. H. Green, *John Wesley*, p. 112
20. Runyon, p. 27. He is referencing Wesley's "The Principles of a Methodist Farther Explained."
21. Knight, p. 168
22. Knight, p. 136, from "The Means of Grace", *The Works of John Wesley*, vol. 1, p.381
23. Runyon, p. 18, from *The Works of John Wesley*, vol. 1, p. 442
24. Robertson Davies, *What's Bred In The Bone*, p. 299

Chapter Four

Born Again Integrity

"How can a grown man be born again?" Nicodemus asked. "He cannot enter his mother's womb and be born a second time!" "I am telling you," replied Jesus, "A person is born physically of human parents, but is born spiritually of the Spirit." (John 3:1-8)

Movies and Life

The movie *The Legend of Bagger Vance* begins just before World War I in Savannah. Rannulf Junuh, played by actor Matt Damon, is the local golden-boy. He is good at golf; good at love with pretty Adele; and by many standards, good at life. Then the war comes. In the horror of battle, all the men in Captain Junuh's unit die. Junuh comes home to Savannah as a sad loner who holes up in his family's run-down estate. Years pass. The Depression comes. And like the entire nation, Savannah suffers.

Resourceful Adele, Junuh's old flame, and now a savvy business person, comes up with a daring plan to boost Savannah's economy and her family's sagging fortune: a celebrity golf match. She charms golf superstars Bobby Jones and Walter Hagen into coming. After all the years, Adele seeks out Junuh and entreats him to compete as the local favorite son. Though he protests he has lost his swing, Adele persists until Junuh reluctantly agrees. In the providence of the story, late one night, a stranger shows up, Bagger Vance, played by Will Smith. Bagger proves to be a sort of Christ figure who coaches Junuh back into golf and life.

To Junuh, who has lost his swing, Bagger speaks of finding his true, authentic swing. Bagger teaches Junuh that his authentic swing is not so much an achievement as it is a gift, that it is not so much figured out in the mind, as it is felt out in the body, that golf is not so much a game to win but to play well. The turning point in the cliffhanger match with Hagen and Jones is when Junuh slices into a dense stand of trees. Deep in the rough, there is only a thin corridor to the green. It is that one stroke or nothing. And Junuh's swing is reborn.

Robert Redford directed this movie, which is based on Stephen Pressfield's book *The Legend of Bagger Vance: A Novel of Golf and the Game of Life.*[1] It is clear that "true authentic swing" equates with whatever it is that gives meaning and joy to our lives, that which makes us most real and alive. To recover, or maybe discover for the first time, the real you and me God made us to be gets us close to the heart of the game of life. Integrity is a factor here: how we find the core values that penetrate the compartments of our lives; how we respond to God's presence in all the people and situations coming at us instead of reacting helter-skelter on our own. What's more, being people of integrity, finding the "true authentic swing" part of us is not so much a matter of gritting our teeth and mustering on as it is discovering the grace, the "beyond our own doing" strength that God gives us, that enlivens and revives us, and the joy of being alive in spite of the complications of our lives.

Late Night with Jesus

Just as Bagger shows up late one night for Junuh, in John 3, a man named Nicodemus comes looking for Jesus by cover of night. We are told that Nicodemus is a prominent leader in the community, a Pharisee. Pharisees took their faith and life seriously. Far from moral slackers, they are depicted by the New Testament to be people who sometimes took doing the right thing in the opposite direction of judgmental extremism. In their own way, they sought to be people of integrity.

In one of his novels, Canadian author Robertson Davies comments that a truly well-dressed man's clothing is so tastefully understated that it is not the first thing you notice about him. I picture Nicodemus well-dressed in that way, with just a bit of distinguishing gray in his dark hair. He slips through Jerusalem to talk with Jesus, the mystic from some podunk place in Galilee called Nazareth. It's a reading between the biblical lines thing, but the impression we get is that Nicodemus has lost his swing, maybe wonders if he ever had it. My sense is that he resembles a lot of us: looking good on the outside, but holding together inside only with extreme effort.

The ravages of war killed off Junuh's swing in golf and life. Sometimes it is the war going on in our relationships, or the war going on inside us, that tank us. Loss of someone we love, an "iffy" illness, or being stuck in some energy-sapping situation—those sorts of things can kill off the part of us that is most real and alive. In the integrity dimension of our lives, even "good" people sometimes do "bad" things. We cross ethical lines in our business. Sacred marriage promises are broken. It's hard to admit that many, if not most, of our wounds are self-inflicted.

Sometimes it's not the big bangs that get us but the day-in and -out holding action of keeping on keeping on. Over lunch one day, a group of us pastor-types got to talking about maintaining a sense of joy and energy in our work, and experiencing our call to ministry as ongoing, not something shrinking ever smaller in the rear view mirror of our memory. One guy said, "To anyone going into the ministry, I always say, 'hold on to your joy. Don't let anyone take away your joy.'" We all agreed that was easier said than done, and that not just pastor-types, but pretty much everyone had this struggle. Someone then brought up church consultant Bill Easum's contention that ministers who want to make a difference in the new century cannot do ministry the same ways we did in the '80s or even the '90s. For ministers and church leaders, it's new forms of worship. Small groups are taking much of the role of traditional Sunday School classes. Many pastoral care conversations now take place by email and text messaging.

Business people, teachers, doctors, builders, managers, students, even parents can't do everything the same way they did just ten years ago and make it. It's a bit scary when experts tell us we need to reinvent ourselves every five years or so. Few get to settle in with one job, one institution, or one location for twenty to thirty years anymore. None of us can put our skill-set on cruise control. It's scary, but it is also exhilarating.

We can fill in our own blanks with what ruins our swing, saps our joy, and undermines our integrity. Who knows exactly what it was with Nicodemus? Maybe, things had not turned out the way he hoped, or maybe they had turned out as he had hoped, but they were not all they were cracked up to be. Whatever the reason, something more than a casual interest in a theological and philosophical chat sent Nicodemus out into the night to talk with Jesus.

Jesus and Nicodemus have what would likely be on many people's top ten list of conversations in the Bible. Jesus talks to Nicodemus about his true authentic swing, that part of him that is most real, as being born again. Lead-headed literalist Nicodemus sputters that stuff about how grown men cannot reenter their mothers' bodies. It must have felt pretty oppressive at first to him. Here he was, seeking help, perhaps desperate for it, and Nicodemus hears that an impossible task is required.

Jesus, the great coach-midwife of life, shakes his head and clarifies that he is talking about the mystery of God's life-changing Spirit. Like wind, the Spirit is an unseen but real power. He offers Nicodemus not the demand to change (a *got to*), but the power to change (a *get to*). Even now, some make being born again a demand. Many, however, discover that being born again is not a task, but a gift from God. God gives this gift not just once but again and again. God's Spirit can empower us to make changes we never could on our own.

Reinvented Integrity

I came across an interview with comedian Jerry Seinfeld in which he discusses a documentary film being made about his efforts to "reinvent" himself, to create new comic material, to move beyond the safe, proven routines that have made him rich and famous. Part of it, he says, started a few years ago in a live performance. As he launched into his monologue, out of the dark from the audience came someone's voice, "Heard it!" He says, "It was like someone throwing a spear . . . through my chest." He continues, "I've kind of graduated from show business . . . . It's not about the money anymore, and it's not about fame. Now, it's just about maintaining a creative arc."

In maintaining a creative arc, there's a joy dimension. Though doing the same thing over and over may be safe, it eventually becomes dull. There's also an integrity dimension. We shortchange others and ourselves when we live more out of our "thens" instead of our "nows." It initially struck me as a heavy task that Seinfeld has set out for himself. He is out scouting around his neighborhood with legal pad in hand, people watching along the sidewalks, in the shops, and in the parks in search of new humor. Being funny is hard work!

Later in the interview, Seinfeld talks about his then almost two-year-old daughter. He says, "I didn't know there was a laugh better than any laugh I had ever heard before. But there is. That one little girl laughing is better than 3,000 people. Since my whole life is about getting a laugh, to have something come along that creates a new category above anything else; that kind of stopped me in my tracks."[2]

Seinfeld is talking about what many of us call the working of God's grace. The gift of a child gives him not just one more demand to reinvent himself, but the energy and joy that empower him to do it. Seeking the new humor becomes not something he has got to do, but something he gets to do.

God's grace comes to us through the "means of grace." Through such ordinary wonders as worship, prayer, beauty, Bible study, people who care about us, people for whom we care, and paying close attention to our lives, God gives us strength to go on, to make those life changes. Big mouths finally listen. Mealy mouths finally speak up. Workaholics give it a rest. Procrastinators get it in gear. Bitter ones forgive and are forgiven. Addicts stick to the program. Greedy ones become generous ones. Grieving ones find joy again. Frightened ones find something stronger than their fear.

Being people of integrity means, of course, telling the truth, not cutting corners with our business and tax returns, keeping our promises (marriage-wise and otherwise), taking responsibility instead of making excuses for our lives. But it is also more: integrity is a way of living in relationship to God that conditions all we say, do, and are. Integrity is the God-given strength to respond to life in relationship to God instead of reacting to things on our own. Nicodemus met the One whose grace gives us the pattern and power to hold or change our course as needed. Living in relationship to God gives us firm values by which we can operate as whole persons and withstand the compartmentalization of life.

A paraphrase of Psalm 1: Blessed are people of integrity. They resist urges to play the game and look out only for number one. They have a passion to find God's good way. They are like deep-rooted trees planted by a river. They flourish in good times and withstand the storms.

Reflection for Spiritual Formation

Reflection One

Read John 3:1-8 quickly. Read it again, this time slowly. Try using a different translation of the story to get beyond the familiar (i.e., Jerusalem Bible, Phillips, Peterson's Translation, etc.) Imagine yourself as Nicodemus, scurrying through the dark streets to see Jesus. What must Nicodemus be feeling as he approaches Jesus in the night? How do you feel as you approach God in prayer? Why do you feel this way? What, if anything, does this tell you about your relationship with God? Write your responses in the space provided.

_____

_____

_____

_____

_____

_____

Prayer

Let this be your breath prayer throughout the day:

O God, you are my God, eagerly I seek you. (Psalm 63:1)

Reflection Two

Read Psalm 1 in its entirety. The author paraphrases Psalm 1:1-3 in this chapter. According to his paraphrase, what is it that people of integrity do in relationship to God and others? Do as the psalmist says and sit quietly and meditate on this passage.

Prayer

Begin your prayer reading these words from Psalm 8:1,3-4:

"O Lord, our Sovereign, how majestic is your name in all the earth...

When I look at your heavens, the work of your fingers,

the moon and stars that you have established;

what are human beings that you are mindful of them, mortals,

that you care for them?"

Great giver of our lives, we are amazed.

As we do our work today, remind us that we live under the canopy of your love.

Enable us to respond, not react, to one another.

Amen.

Reflection Three

In this chapter, the author talks about reinventing ourselves in our work or lives. We do this to keep our "creative arc." He also describes joy-sapping work or life events. We sometimes must reinvent ourselves to restore or even find joy. Where do you find joy? Take a moment and meditate on your joy. Find a reminder of it. For example, it might be a shell from the beach or a hair ribbon or a photograph. Keep the reminder in your sacred space or somewhere else to remind you of your joy. Write your responses in the space provided or in a journal.

_____

_____

_____

_____

_____

_____

_____

_____

Prayer

Sing praises to the Lord, O you his faithful ones,
and give thanks to his holy name.
For his anger is but for a moment; his favor is for a lifetime.
Weeping may linger for the night,
but joy comes with the morning.
Psalm 30:4-5

Add this line to the verses above and say them together as a prayer:

"O God, in you my joy is complete. Amen."

CHAPTER FOUR NOTES
1. Robert Redford, Director, "The Legend of Bagger Vance"
2. Rick Lyman, "Going Hunting in Seinfeld Country: Just For Laughs," New York Times, September 15, 2002

Chapter Five

Integrity in a Passionate World

Jesus came to a well. A Samaritan woman came to draw water. Jesus said, "Give me some water." The woman answered, "You are a Jew and I am a Samaritan, so how can you ask me?" Jesus answered, "If you only knew who it is asking you . . . you would have asked him and he would have given you living water. "The woman said to him, "Sir, you have no bucket and the well is deep. Where do you get that living water?" (John 4: 4-42)

A Man and a Woman

Monica Lewinsky is not quite the household name it was a few years ago. Yet for a time, accounts of what had or had not happened between the young White House intern and the then President dominated the media. Some might debate whether the enormity of the scandal was reached when it played a part in the impeachment proceedings of the President or when it led to that pinnacle achievement in our celebrity driven time: a Barbara Walters' television interview of Ms. Lewinsky.

No laughing matter, it was not the first nor the last time alleged sexual misbehavior of a political leader cast a shadow across the integrity of all leaders. As the Monica matter unfolded, some of the President's congressional accusers were discovered to be guilty of infidelity. Nationally and locally known religious leaders at times join the ranks of those discovered crossing the line of ethical integrity with their sexual activity. The reputed sexual high jinks of stars and celebrities continue to intrigue us more than we'd like to admit. Sexuality is deeply rooted in human beings, both male and female.

In John 4, there is a lengthy conversation between, Jesus and an unnamed Samaritan woman he meets at her village well. Somehow, Jesus knows that she has had five husbands and a current live-in. At times, preacher-types are known to depict her as a Samaritan shady lady, or at least a passionate practitioner of marathon serial marriage. But it may be high time to chunk this caricature. According to Biblical Professor Gail O'Day in The New Interpreter's Bible Commentary, this provocative depiction is likely inaccurate.[1] By the practices of that day, only men could initiate or leave marriages. The indications are that this woman was less a vamp or vixen and more a victim. After all, there were at least six men in this situation whose ethics are also in question. (And without going too far away from this passage, ahead in John 8, there is the account of a woman caught in the act of adultery who was brought before a crowd for stoning. What about the man in this act of adultery?)

So, whether the specifics of the Samaritan woman's life were PG or R Rated, Jesus speaks with her about not only physical water for which both were thirsty but also about "spiritual water" for which all of us thirst. We human being are not finely compartmentalized creatures. Our physical, mental, and spiritual dimensions are a swirl of inter-relatedness. Our physical passions express not only the hungers of our hormones but also the hungers of our hearts.

Our words *passion* and *passionate* are multifaceted. Those words express a number of realities that are both related to and in tension with one another. To say someone is a passionate person can mean anything from having a volatile temper, to getting very emotional, to having a strong sensual/sexual desire; from caring deeply about a matter, to having intense energy, devotion, and love for a cause—even for Christ and life itself. We speak at times of the passion of Christ: his deep love and suffering for the world and us, particularly by his cruciform suffering and death for us. Passion is not a steady-as-she-goes matter. Passion expresses the intensities of the agonies and ecstasies of life. Passion defies life as a spectator-sport; it reaches, cries, and laughs out for participation, connection, relationship, and involvement with each other, with life, with God.

Let me offer a start on a working definition of passion: *Passion is the God given physical-emotional-mental-spiritual hunger and energy we have to be connected, related, and involved with more than ourselves.* The God of Genesis did not want to be alone and in our created reflectedness of God, we do not want to be alone either. Our passion for love and life is not a curse but a gift. Yet as the energy that holds atoms and us together can become explosively destructive when turned against itself, the life energy of our passions when misused can destroy the very relationships and joy we seek.

We are exploring *integrity*: living rightly, living from a moral/spiritual center. Once again, our working definition of integrity is: *the God given strength to respond to our lives in relationship to God instead of reacting to things on our own.* To be a Christian does not require a "passion-ectomy!" Anything but. Our passion for living and loving connects us with the God we are to love with our whole hearts, minds, souls, and strength. That passion connects us with those around us whom we are to love as ourselves. When it comes to sexual expression, we need all the help we can get from God and each other to respond instead of react to each other somehow in relation to God and not use one another as mere gratifying means to our ends.

Veteran actors Ossie Davis and Ruby Dee had one of the magnificent minorities of show-business marriages: it was life-long. In some reading, I came across a wise, witty comment Davis made about marriage. "I say to my fellow husbands whose eyes may be covered with lust. The way to know all women is to know one woman well."[2] Those words remind me of the so-called "Biblical marital motto" found throughout the Bible in the Old Testament, the Gospels, and in the Epistles: the two will become one.[3] (Ephesians 5:31)

As in most areas of life, there is a host of mitigating and extenuating circumstances related to sexual expression. While there is no room for taking sexual advantage of a child or of a subordinate by one in power, our society and church continues to struggle with same-sex relationships. Strong arguments are made from both sides using physiological, psychological, and sociological data; as well as on philosophical and theological grounds. What's more, this is no mere abstract, armchair "interesting" conversation. We are talking about real people, many of whom are known to and loved by us.

What are we to say to this? We live in a complex world. We follow a Jesus who continues to be more inclusive in his love than his followers are. We follow a Jesus who accepts us all but does not approve of all we do. Based on biblical grounds, the teaching of the church over the centuries, and the debated yet overall witness of human experience, our United Methodist *Discipline* reserves its full affirmation of sexual expression for the relationship of a man and a woman in marriage. "Fidelity in marriage and celibacy in singleness" is the phrase often heard. This is one ongoing side of this equation.[4]

Yet the other side of the equation comes from what might be called an appropriate "Gospel tension" in our church's disciplinary position. All people, no exceptions, are included in the grace of God; included, indeed wanted and needed, in the hospitality, family, pastoral care, and shared ministries of the church. Homosexual persons are specifically identified. Though all of our sincere attempts to reach out to others, to share love, to connect, and to be in relationship with other human beings express in fitting ways God's good gift of passion, the church cannot condone all *expressions*, even as it seeks to include all *persons* in its care. (Including in its care even those of us who are convicted by the far more numerous biblical passages inveighing against gluttony, greed, and hardheartedness toward the poor!)

Most of us can attest that even in the most conventional, accepted lifestyles, sexuality is a complicated matter. It is hard to be as sensitive, patient, tender, unselfish, and open as we want to be. At times, there is almost a desire to regain a lost innocence, to have a chance to start over. That feeling of wishing we could get the toothpaste back into the tube extends to the way we treat and are treated by people, to the way we do our work and approach life. Is there a way to get to something that we cannot go back to?

Like a Virgin

"It's Never Too Late To Be a Virgin," was the heading of a New York Times article, subtitled, "No more sex till the wedding, some brides-to-be say."

Reporter Elizabeth Hayt chronicled what she described as a growing trend, particularly across the South, of "secondary virginity." It's something of an "accommodation to the modern reality of premarital sex and the traditional disapproval of it in the Bible belt."[5] Couples who have been sexually active agree to stop having sex for several weeks or months or even a year before they marry. Reasons given to Ms. Hayt by those she interviewed include those wanting to insure "sparks fly on the honeymoon," to wanting to connect somehow with the expectations of family and the church that sex is reserved for marriage, to recapturing a sense of purity, even innocence.

There is a bit of tongue-in-cheek irony in the article to be sure. You either are or are not a virgin say our clinical/literal minds! But hold on. In the exquisite relatedness of all the parts of our lives, I believe this "second virginity" notion is both about sex and about more than sexual activity. Our sexual passion for intensity and connectedness beyond ourselves is a *part* of our hunger for love, completeness, and relationship with other persons and with God. Our passion is a hunger for excitement, energy, joy, and meaning in our lives. That passion gets expressed in our drive to succeed, to be somebody, to make our mark, to win, to fill whatever it is inside us that feels empty. This shows up in our relationships with people, the way we do our work and play, our use of money, and how we deal with the "God thing" in our lives.

Thus, our passion and drive for more of all this causes us to reach out to experience more of the fullness of life. Yet our passions can also cause us to go too fast and too far, to overexpose ourselves, to feel that we have seen too much and done too much, that we have used and been used too much. A kind of "passion burnout" can set in. Too much of a "been there-done that" attitude can issue in a cockiness or cynicism or "passion boredom" that concludes that not much remains to enliven us. What's more, the sense that we have gone too far, and done too much can create old-fashioned guilt and shame, and a wish that we could try again. There may well be a connection among all those things we do to start over: new year's resolutions, new jobs, new homes, new relationships, entry and reentry into church participation, new diets and exercise regimens, even the seemingly oxymoronic 'secondary virginity'.

In *The Shattered Lantern: Rediscovering a Felt Presence of God*, Ronald

Rolheiser describes a spiritual process he calls "revirginization." He clarifies that this new virginity is not so much related to past sexual activity as it expresses a new way of living our lives. Revirginization addresses "the tiredness of soul" that comes with "the greatest of all illusions, the illusion of familiarity." This "virginal spirit" or "revirginization" suggests a paradoxical return to somewhere we have both been and never been. Rohlheiser connects this with what has been called "second naiveté." "Revirginization refers to a process of continually recapturing the posture of a child before reality. Second naiveté describes that posture, as it exists in an adult who has moved beyond the natural naiveté of a child, but who is not fixated in the deserts of cynicism, criticism, and false sophistication."[6]

To "revirginize" in this case means to recover the "ancient instinct for astonishment", to be able to be amazed again at the wonders all around us: the beauty of the world, the mystery of a person, the sheer enigma that we get to live at all. There is a sort of abiding "holy incompleteness" to what we know about ourselves, each other, life, and God. To be surprised again is one of God's precious gifts.

As a pastor, I have witnessed a number of "revirginization miracles." One day, I visited with Millie. Until a rare illness almost took her life, Millie had been a bright, active person in the church and community: small business owner, busy wife, mother, and grandmother, as well as a daughter who kept a close eye on her aged mother. There had been several long weeks in the hospital during which it was far from certain that Millie would ever come home. But she did. The day we visited in her den, she was at long last returning to health. She said, "It's the strangest thing. We've lived here for years, but now when I look out the window at my backyard, it's different. I look at the grass, the flowers, the sky. Now, green is greener, red is redder, and blue is bluer than ever before. It's like I'm really seeing the world for the first time."

I have been married to my wife for thirty-plus years. We have our ups, downs, and middles. She knows me so well it scares me at times, and she has given me the gift of knowing a lot about her. Still, the miracle of "revirginization" still strikes me time and again. She says something or does something and I realize what a mystery she is, that I don't and won't ever have her figured out.

The competence she brings to her work, her faithful caring for me, her children, family and friends far exceeds my capacities. The emotional, physical, mental, and spiritual intertwining of our lives is an enlivening mix of familiarity and surprise. That we have this love continues to astonish me more than ever.

Faithful expression of our passions happen in renewed commitment to fidelity and in renewed commitment to at least seasons of celibacy. Again, the capacity to live with a virginal spirit, the ongoing process of revirginization, goes far beyond our sexual activity. Overall, living with integrity in a passionate world is discovering anew that all our passions are related and connected finally to God, who alone can completely complete us.

A Passion for Integrity

Preachers, religious writers, and such have almost worn a hole in the words of fourth-century theologian Augustine: "God, you have made us for yourself, and our hearts are restless until they find their rest in you." Our passion and hunger for the people, possessions, experiences, and relationships of our lives will always fall short and be incomplete until they are *connected* to and *corrected* by God, the great giver and saver of our lives.

To the Athenians, Paul spoke of God as the "one in whom we live and move and have our being." (Acts 17:28) The theologian H. Richard Niebuhr referred to God as the "One beyond the many" to whom we respond in and through all our relationships and experiences. A passion for integrity does not cancel out the wonderful network of people and causes in our lives and take us to some unworldly place where we commune only with God. This passion puts our web of life into a broader and deeper context, so that all we have and do are reframed in relationship with the great mystery of God present in all these parts of our lives.

Thus, connecting our sexuality with God, the giver of this and all good gifts, causes us to express and enjoy it in a faithful, people-cherishing way, and corrects us from expressing it in a superficial, people-using way.

Integrity, in this sense, also extends to our passion for money, success, meaning, and recognition. It's said that money is a terrible master but a wonderful servant. Money used only for our own accumulation and gratification becomes a greedy matter. Money connected to and corrected by the great gift giver supports our families, contributes to those who are at risk in the world, undergirds churches, schools, and 1,001 other people and earth saving efforts.

The unchecked passion to be "somebody" can issue into the catastrophic egomania of a Hitler, or into the daily damage of the self-absorbed-self-promoting "little Hitlers" we can become. That passion to be someone significant can have the world impact of the humanitarian life of a Jimmy Carter or in the impact on our little worlds by the daily variety of saints in our midst: teachers, friends, mentors, and the host of people who do their work with people-centered, caring competence.

Passion is a God given gift, a hunger to live life to its fullest, to connect and reach beyond ourselves to something more than ourselves. Such passion for life is not dampened and stifled by the God of Jesus Christ; it is grounded in and supercharged by God's love. In his *The Passion for Life: A Messianic Lifestyle*, German theologian Jurgen Moltmann writes:

> In the passion of Christ I see the passion of God himself and discover again the passion of my own heart . . . Jesus' life is inspired not just by the wish for life *after* death, but by the will for life *before* death, yes, even *against* death.[7] Edward Beck concludes his *God Underneath: Spiritual Memoirs of a Catholic Priest* with some reflections on those famous, often repeated words of Augustine. As I pray in a faith community, we believe in a power and richness beyond ourselves—a love born of desire that transcends the physical and rises above what we can see, feel, taste, and touch . . . . In the end, what has really mattered? To what have we given our lives? With whom have we cast our lot? Whom have we loved—really loved? I'm not sure much else matters.[8]

The Samaritan woman experiences Jesus as a man who really looks, not leers, at her. He sees the more to her than meets the eye. She rushes into the village and says to the others, "Come and see a man who told me everything I have ever done!" (John 4:29) Someone has said that it's as if she is saying, "He knows all about me and still loves me." Now, she begins to discover that there is more to her and her life than she ever knew, that her life is connected to more than the daily trips to the well and the nightly grasps of ones who may leave, neither of which finally quench her thirst and fill her emptiness on their own. Maybe she remembered David's words in Psalm 51 after Nathan challenged his behavior with Bathsheba: "Create in me a clean heart, O God, and renew a right spirit within me." Because of this Jesus, all of us thirsty, passionate people can experience ourselves connected to the life-giving/life-saving mystery whom we call God, and discover ourselves and one another as whole and holy again, or perhaps for the first time, after all.

For Spiritual Reflection

Reflection One

In chapter 2, the author talked about "operational little gods" that get in the way of discernment. In this chapter, he tells us our passions for worldly things get in the way of our passion for God. Reflect for a moment on those things you are passionate about, using the author's definition of passion in this chapter. What are they? Do they keep you from being passionate about God? If so, how? How might your worldly passions enhance or energize your passion for God? Write your responses in the space provided or in your journal.

_____

_____

_____

_____

Prayer

For the next twenty-four hours, let this breath prayer be your focus.

God of dreams, fill me with excitement.

Reflection Two

Read Psalm 139:13-18. The author reminds us we are made in God's image. (Genesis 1:26) Quietly reflect on how wonderfully we are made and what it means to you to be made in God's image. Write a prayer expressing your reflection.

Prayer

Pray Psalm 139:13-18 as your prayer today.

For it was you who formed my inward parts;
   you knit me together in my mother's womb.
I praise you, for I am fearfully and wonderfully made.
   Wonderful are your works; that I know very well.
My frame was not hidden from you, when I was being made in secret,
   intricately woven in the depths of the earth.
Your eyes beheld my unformed substance.
In your book were written all the days that were formed for me,
   when none of them as yet existed.
How weighty to me are your thoughts, O God!
I try to count them—they are more than the sand:
   I come to the end—I am still with you. Amen.

Reflection Three

Re-read the first two paragraphs under the heading "Like a Virgin." Has there been a time in your life when your "physical passion" got beyond you and damaged a human relationship in your life? If not, what kept your passion in check?

If so, is there anything that can be done to reconcile the situation? If there isn't anything that can be done, can you accept that and ask for forgiveness?

Can you forgive yourself?

On a separate sheet of paper, write a letter to someone you've hurt, asking for forgiveness. Then tear up the letter and "give" it to God.

Prayer

Read Psalm 51

Through the day use words from verse 10 as a breath prayer:

Create in me a clean heart, O God, and give me a new spirit.

CHAPTER FIVE NOTES

1. Gail O'Day, *The New Interpreter's Bible*, vol. IX (9), p. 567
2. This quote is from a New York Times book review of a book by Ossie Davis.
3. Genesis 2, 24; Mark 10:6f.; Ephesians 6:31
4. *United Methodist Discipline*, 2004, p. 161 (par. G); p. 162 (par. H & S)
5. Elizabeth Hayt, "It's Never Too Late To Be A Virgin," New York Times, August 4, 2002, Section 9, pp. 1 & 6
6. Ronald Rohlheiser, *The Shattered Lantern: Rediscovering a Felt Presence of God*, p. 190
7. Jurgen Moltmann, *A Passion for Life: A Messianic Lifestyle*, p. 24
8. Edward Beck, *God Underneath: The Spiritual Memoirs of a Catholic Priest*, p. 231

.

Chapter Six

Integrity Vision

"One thing I know. I was blind and now I see." "If you were blind then you would not be guilty. But since you claim that you can see, this means that you are guilty." (John 9:1-41)

Seeing What We Are Looking For

When our children were in high school, there was a zealous assistant principal who we will call Mr. Payne. Mr. Payne was in charge of student discipline and behavior matters at the large 2,000+ population school. At some time during his tenure, Mr. Payne was on crutches, his broken ankle in a cast. It seems that in Mr. Payne's beyond-the-call-of-duty surveillance of student behavior, he had fallen out of a tree. It was revealed that Mr. Payne had taken to hiding in trees near the student parking lot during the lunch hours. His mission was to detect which students were slipping out to the parking lot to smoke, kiss, or Burger King it for lunch. Apparently, as he juggled his pen, pad, and binoculars, he lost his hold and fell, fracturing his ankle and perhaps a bit of his pride.

I overheard a conversation some of the youth of our church were having about Mr. Payne's misadventure. One student said, "I'm not saying it's okay to slip out of school during lunch hour, but I wish Mr. Payne would work just half as hard to see the good things we do as he does to catch us breaking the rules."

In John 9, there is a fascinating story of Jesus' encounter with blindness. On the surface, it's a story of a blind man being given his sight. It is that, but it's also more. It's about the blindness of a lot of people, the least of them being the man who was born physically blind. The disciples see this blind (sightless) man but are themselves blind (clueless) to a fellow human who needs compassion. What they "see" is a chance to have an interesting theological conversation about how, why, and if God punishes people, and about who is to blame and for what. The religious rule-and-score-keepers present are blind to God's astonishing love at work with the man's restoration of sight. All they "see" is this who-does-he-think-he-is guy, Jesus, breaking their don't-work-on-the-Sabbath blue laws.

A case can be made for saying that we are all blind from birth. As Jesus told Nicodemus, we need to be born again and anew to see ourselves, each other, and our world in the light of God's love. We can have a sort of 20/20 blindness that only sees what we want to see. Our 20/20 blindness sees clearly what is rotten in other people's lives but misses what is out of whack in our own. If people don't pass our litmus tests—on religion, politics, letting us have our way, or whatever—then we don't 'see' much good in them. Our post 9/11 world is even more dangerous because so many on both sides want to see all the evil and blame in the other side without accounting for their own faults. We may have acute sight when it comes to the raw deals in our lives, but be bat-blind to our blessings. It's so hard to see what's good, or at least understandable, in the jerks and adversaries of our lives.

Jesus speaks chilling words to people who practice the selective vision of seeing only what they want to see. The refusal to see what God puts in front of our faces creates a lot of grief for us and the people who have to put up with us.

We have been operating with the working definition of integrity as *the God given strength to respond to life in relationship to God instead of reacting to things on our own*. For now, I suggest a related working definition for what might be called "integrity vision." *Integrity vision is the God given capacity to see the God-connection between us and the people-situations of our lives*. Such grace-focused vision enables us to "sight" the presence of God in the predicaments and relationships of our lives. John Wesley spoke of the "means of grace." These are the ordinary and extraordinary ways such strength and vision come to us through worship, prayer, study, relationships, caring acts, and paying attention to the more-than-meets-the-eye things that go on before our very eyes.

Eskimo Sightings

In her delightfuly quirky book *Traveling Mercies*, Anne Lamott shares a story about a bush pilot in Alaska. The pilot recounts his harrowing experience of his plane crashing in the icy tundra and how the ordeal has caused him to lose his faith. Bitterly, he tells of being stuck in the plane for hours, getting ever colder, praying as hard as he could for God to help him. But, he says, God didn't do a thing, so he's had it with the God business. A bit baffled, the listener counters, "Still, after all that, you survived, you're here!" "Oh, yeah, that," shrugged the pilot, "only because some *#*#*# Eskimo finally came along."[1]

The account of the blind man healed and all its complications go on a long time in John 9. Most of the time, Jesus is "offstage." Indeed, this is the longest stretch in John's Gospel without Jesus front and center. We have already mentioned how so many failed to see God's love at work with the man's new sight. Let's not be too hard on those characters in John's story. Seldom are there giant sound speakers blaring and video screens flashing HERE IS GOD'S LOVE AND PRESENCE AT WORK IN YOUR LIFE NOW!!! God is a little subtler, a little more respectful of our freedom, a little more offstage than that. But God's Eskimos do come.

Don't mistake this for little more than a positive attitude song and dance routine. "Just put on our positive attitude glasses, and we will see that all our messes are really wonderful things . . . . yada-yada!" Still, Jesus does help us see more of God's love at work in our lives than we spot on first glance. How amazing! Even imperfect people with their own share of complications do, after all, love us, put up with us, even sacrifice for us. Driving along on a chilly spring morning, the sight of some in-your-face yellow daffodils remind you of your grandmother's daffodils years ago and her love that yet abides with you. Grief, illness, depression, and stress burden people, but somehow they/we go on. From where does such marvelous, mysterious strength to do as well as we do come? Are we so myopic to think that God is not involved, that some Eskimo just happened along?

Eye Exercises

From early childhood my eyeglasses have been the thing first put on in the morning and last thing taken off at bedtime. My staple response to being called four-eyes at school was, "Yeah, well, four eyes are better than two," though I don't think they or I were convinced of that. For a couple of years when I was a little boy, I had to do various eye-strengthening exercises. Despite my parents cajoling me that wearing a patch over one eye to strengthen the other was cool like a pirate, I didn't find it much fun. There also were some eye chart reading exercises I had to do with a sort of "view master" gizmo. All of this was interspersed with regular trips to have my eyes tested, when I, with dilated owl-eyes, looked at the chart as Dr. Miles flipped different lens in front of my eyes saying, "Billy, is this better or worse . . . better or worse . . . ?

There are no gimmicks for Integrity Vision—the capacity to see God connected with the people and situations of our lives. But there just might be some spiritual eye exercises, simple spiritual disciplines, than can help. The "What would Jesus do?" practice is a sort of an Integrity Vision exercise. To answer that question we have to "see" our situation in light of what we know about the pattern of life Jesus gives us.

Perhaps, we might strive to look at things through Mother Teresa Eyes. When asked how she worked with and touched the poor, sick, and dying people of Calcutta day in and out, the world- treasure nun gave her often quoted yet profound answer that she saw Jesus in them. This follows from Matthew 25's parable of the Last Judgment, where Jesus says how we treat the least important person who is in need is as if we did or did not do it to him. All we know about Jesus from the gospels indicate that this "least" person extends to the enemy and the ones we consider absolutely the least likely to be Christ bearing. With the person who is complicating our life, the one who drives us up the wall, the person or group that is so "not our kind of people" that we find them repugnant, it is no easy task to see them with Mother Teresa Eyes, to see them somehow as Christ bearing. It takes vision of great integrity to see such people somehow connected to God, to respond to them accordingly, and not to react to them on our own.

Along the way, I came across a little phrase that has application to our eye exercises for Integrity Vision: See Jesus at your side; then decide. By this, I do not mean to suggest that Christian decision making and living can be reduced to some catchy phrase or simplistic formula. Yet such a sentence can quickly distill what is at stake in our decisions and our treatment of people. Whereas Mother Teresa Eyes cause me to see Christ in the person I am dealing with, this practice causes me to picture Christ standing beside me, encouraging, guiding, pulling for me as I frame my words and actions.

All three of these "eye exercises" are, of course, easier said than done. Not every moral, faithful person will "see" the same thing. We have to remind ourselves that "seeing" people as Jesus would see them does not mean a sort of mushy, sentimental sweetness that approves of whatever they want to do. With his great "Yeses" came also some thundering "Nos". His way usually makes us hold one another more accountable; causes us to get involved in complicated situations, and not blithely bless things from a comfortable distance. Integrity Vision doesn't mean that every little decision has to be some spiritual ordeal (Italian or Chinese for dinner? Boots or tennis shoes today?) But I do mean we begin to see God's love blessing what's good in our lives and hurting with us in the messes. I do mean simply, but not easily, seeing the relationship between God's love in Jesus and how we operate in our lives.

Sights for Sore Eyes

At one point in his book, *Summer of 49*, David Halberstam writes about the Yankee Clipper Joe DiMaggio: He was ever conscious of his obligation to play well. Late in his career, when his legs were bothering him and the Yankees had a comfortable lead in a pennant race, a friend of his asked him why he played so hard. The games, after all, no longer meant so much. "'Because there might be someone out there who's never seen me play before,' he answered."[2]

Thus far, we have talked a great deal about what *we* see, how we see Jesus present in the people and situations of our lives, how we might picture Jesus standing beside us encouraging us to see the God connection between ourselves and what we are doing. All that is crucial. DiMaggio's words bring one other critical dimension of seeing to us. That is, just who and what do people see in *us*? This is a trembly prospect. But your and my life might be the sight of God's love for somebody's sore eyes. After all, we learn about the forgiveness of God through the forgiveness of others. We learn about God's love that doesn't give up on us through people who do not give up on us. We learn about the beautiful heart of God through the beautiful hearts of certain people. Integrity Vision, then, is not just looking for God's love and presence out there around us, but living so that perhaps a few people might catch a glimpse of God's love for them and the world in us.

Try this breath prayer for a few days:

God, help me be your Eskimo in a few people's lives. Amen.

For Spiritual Reflection

Reflection One

Read John 9:1-41 quickly. Read it again, this time slowly, savoring the words as you read them. Imagine yourself as one of the members of the crowd. What is your reaction to the blind man's restoration of sight? What are your "blind spots" in your relationship to God? What is God saying to you in these words regarding integrity as a response in relationship to God? Write your responses in the space provided or in a journal.

_____

_____

_____

_____

_____

_____

Prayer

Let this breath prayer guide you for the next twenty-four hours:

Be thou my vision, O God of my heart

Reflection Two

The author reminds us of the definition of integrity as response instead of reaction and then defines "integrity vision" as the "God-given capacity to see the God-connection between us and the people and situation in our lives." Draw a triangle with the three sides of equal length and one of the angles on top. Outside and on top of the top angle, write "God." Outside one of the other angles, write your name. Outside the third angle write "others." This represents your relationship with God and others—you are all connected.

Now draw the triangle so that your side of the triangle gets shorter as you get closer to God. The triangle is no longer equilateral, is it? It's lopsided.

Now shorten the side of the triangle marked "others" so that it is the same length and same distance from God. You still do not have an equilateral triangle, do you? You will have to shorten the line between you and "others" in order for the three sides to remain equal in length.

As you get closer in relationship to God, you get closer in relationship to others.

Now rework the triangle and at "others" put the name of someone you may have trouble "seeing." Are they too far away for you to "see?" Remember that they, too, are connected to God.

Prayer

Using the directives introduced in chapter 1, pray for this "other" you have trouble seeing.

Reflection Three

We've talked about works of mercy. Gather old eyeglasses from your neighbors or friends and then donate them to the Lion's Club or some other organization to use. How does this help you understand integrity vision as seeing "the God-connection between us" and the people who need glasses but can't afford them? Write your reflections in the space provided or in a journal.

_____

_____

_____

_____

_____

Prayer

The author uses this saying: "See Jesus at your side, then decide." As you pray this prayer attributed to St. Patrick (c. 389-461), imagine Jesus all around and in you.

Christ be with me, Christ be within me,
Christ behind me, Christ before me,
Christ beside me, Christ to win me,
Christ to comfort and restore me,
Christ beneath me, Christ above me,
Christ in quiet, Christ in danger,
Christ in hearts of all that love me,
Christ in the mouth of friend and stranger.

CHAPTER SIX NOTES

1. Anne Lamott, *Traveling Mercies*, p. 117
2. David Halberstam, *Summer of '49*, p. 47

Outlive your Life - Max Lucado

The Book of Acts.

　　May 2 → 6 weeks

Chapter Seven

Integrity & Our Life Work

Integrity is the God given strength to *respond* to life in relationship to God instead of *reacting* to things on our own.

Integrity: Operating from firm values. A state of being whole, undivided

It's Gotta Be a Calling

After some icy wintry weather, my car was coated in a crust of dried, dirty slush. It was still too cold to wash the car myself, so I was among the many who showed up at the carwash/detailing place. My glasses instantly fogged as I entered the over-heated waiting area, feet squishing across the ancient shag carpet that was sopping wet from a busted hot water heater.

It was a pandemonious place. The phone was jangling. Customers and workers were swarming in the cramped area. Plumbers, working on the water heater, went back and forth. In the midst of it all, there was Mr. Carwash, the owner-manager. Talking on the phone, answering customer questions, giving workers directions, and hurrying the plumbers, he was a busy man.

After getting my car wash lined up with Mr. Carwash, I edged over to the tiny waiting area in the corner with the ancient *Reader's Digest*s and *Field &*

Streams. Lying low in the corner, I heard the man apparently talking to himself between his negotiations. It was a sort of breath prayer/self pep talk. "Lord, help me. Lord, you know for anybody to do this job, it's gotta be a calling. Lord, I couldn't do this if you hadn't called me to it." More about this man later!

Long before carwashes, Samuel was a great prophet in ancient Israel. He announced God's choice of Saul, and later, David, as kings, the advising of whom was never easy. For Samuel, it began even earlier when, as a gawky adolescent, he heard a voice calling his name in the night. Three times he heard it. Each time he thought it was old Eli the prophet with whom young Samuel stayed in the Temple. Eli counseled his young protégée: "Go, lie down, and if the Lord calls you say, 'Speak, Lord, for your servant is listening.'" (1 Samuel 3:1-10)

Not quite as long ago, but also long before carwashes, Jesus walked along the shore of the Sea of Galilee. He spotted those fishermen: Andrew, Simon, James, and John. He called them to follow him to a new way of life, to minister to the hurts and hopes of people. Amazingly, those guys heard Jesus' call, left it all, and traveled with him (Mark 1:16-20). Because they did so, we are here today as followers of Jesus with joy for living, love for serving, and hope for dying that he gives us. But . . .

However, not everyone, thank God, left town to follow Jesus. Some stayed in town to raise the children, get in the crops, tend the sick, fix the leaky roof, and carry on the life of the community. Thank God for those who went, both then and now, on the road with Jesus. Thank God, too, for those, both then and now, who follow Jesus faithfully right where they are.

Lest we relegate a calling to Bible stories, preacher-rabbi types, or humanitarians, recall that beneath the surface of our secular words *vocation* and *profession* is a sacred core. A *vocation* originally referred to a calling from God to do something with one's life. Profession began as one's profession of faith by dedication of one's life to serving God.

In a world where some are too chummy with God and others too dismissive of God, I suggest this: We humans are aware that there is more than meets the eye in both the world around us and inside us. We sense that there is more to the world around us than the sum of its microchips, critters, rocks, trees, Buicks, and bathtubs. We likewise find that the world inside us is more than the sum of our protoplasmic parts and cerebral circuitry. Experiencing the hints of this connection between the mysterious "more" around us and within us is part of the foundation for hearing a calling and finding meaning for our lives, and is a large part of our quest for integrity in our lives.

The theologian H. Richard Niebuhr portrayed integrity as responding in all the situations of our lives if not directly, then at least indirectly, as responding to God, the One beyond the many, the One somehow present in the many. A sense of call and integrity moves us beyond the false dichotomy between either serving God with my life *or* serving all of the causes, claims, and people swirling in my life. There is still great challenge when we reframe it, but the possibilities that emerge are encouraging if we do so. By God's grace, we seek to find the pattern and power to serve God and hear God's call often *through*, instead of in opposition to, the situations and relationships of our lives. Deciphering God's call in our lives can give us that wholeness and integrity that make it all worthwhile.

United Methodists, along with many other Christians, believe in what is called the "priesthood of all believers" (sometimes called the "general ministry of all Christians.") We believe that all Christians are called by God to be channels of God's love through the lives we live on the job, at home, at church, and in the community. The word "minister" comes from the Latin word *ministerium*, which expresses the New Testament Greek word *diaconos* (deacon), originally referring to a servant who brings food and nourishment to people. The ordination to ministry for Christians is baptism. In the fullness and mystery of it all, Jesus now calls you and me. Baptism is a sacrament of *integrity*, claiming and connecting all of who we are and what we do to God in Jesus Christ.

I have witnessed many who lived such callings. My grandmother ministered to bodies and souls through food, well prepared and lovingly served. I have a friend who is a gifted college professor but whose real passion is the girls' softball league he directs that teaches teens about self-confidence and cooperation with others. My mechanic is a church-going man, but what I most appreciate about him is that he practices "brake ministry." For a fair price, he does good work on my cars that helps get my loved ones and me safely home. My family physician treats me like a whole person not just a symptom sitting on the exam table, and even has a way of making edgy patients like me feel better by just walking into the room. Even in the pandemonium of the mega-discount store I grudgingly go to on occasion, there is a cashier or two who treat me like a human being instead of a hunk of aging protoplasm with a debit card. I pray that more and more people have a sense of serving God through their jobs, community work, and families.

Remember Mr. Carwash? I later found out he intentionally employs only at-risk young adults, to whom he not only gives a job washing cars, but also a chance to clean up their lives. He has several products: clean cars, cleaned up lives, and a redeveloped business in a transitional part of town. From this, he and his employees receive income for themselves and their families. He has stresses galore: equipment that breaks down, cranky customers, and new-to-the-work-force employees. He himself likely has a family, health, or other such issue going on. Yet he perceives that through it all he is responding to One who has called him to this work. The result is a life of integrity and wholeness. "Lord, you know for anybody to do this job, it's gotta be a calling. I couldn't do it if you hadn't called me to it." Indeed.

Deciphering Our Calling

The truth is that most of us do not experience the Mystery calling our name in the night. In her book *The Preaching Life*, Barbara Brown Taylor observes: "What many are missing in their lives is a sense of vocation. In religious language, it means participation in the work of God, something that few people believe they do. Immersed in the corporate worlds of business and finance, and in the domestic worlds of household and family, it is hard for them to see how their lives have anything to do with God."[1]

From time to time, I am asked to speak to older youth and graduates about deciding what to do with their lives, and/or choosing a profession. Sometimes, it is a one-on-one conversation with a young person struggling with what he or she wants to do and what he or she is "expected" to do. Often, I suggest a three-question process to guide their exploration.

- One, what do you like to do, that you are pretty good at, and could, with practice, even be excellent at? Music, computers, relating to people, figuring out things, fixing things, making money, or making dinner, whatever. On a deeper level, these are expressions of our spiritual gifts.

- Two, with work or volunteer service, can you imagine doing this thing that you enjoy in some job or form that helps other people live their lives, that relieves hurt, that increases beauty, that protects the earth?

- Three, is the doing of this thing that you enjoy something that can build up people and/or the earth something that can honor and serve the life-giving mystery who we call God and know through Jesus?

By weaving together our responses to these three questions, we may begin to discover our calling. It is an integrity response, a way of connecting our talents and what we like to do with God's claim on and presence in our lives.

Barbara Brown Taylor relates how her struggle with her decision to become a minister was relieved when she realized that it was a *get to*, not a *got to*, to be a minister. She writes:

> One midnight, I asked God what I was supposed to do. "Anything that pleases you." That was the answer that came into my sleepy head. "What?" I said waking up. "What kind of answer is that?" "Do anything that pleases you," the voice in my head said again, "and belong to me." That simplified things. I could pump gas in Idaho or dig latrines in Pago Pago as long as I remembered whose I was.[2]

The Bridge From Sunday to Monday

Some years ago, I came across then steel industry executive William Diehl's *Thank God, It's Monday!* In this book, Diehl explores how being a Christian is not so much about the things we do on Sundays as it is about the way we go about our jobs and lives in the Monday weekday world.

> The local congregation is not supposed to be terminal in God's purpose; it is supposed to be instrumental. It is not supposed to exist as end in itself, but as a means to an end. The local congregations is where the people of God gather around Word and Sacrament, for praise and prayer, for education and fellowship, and for stimulation and support SO THAT they can scatter into the world on Monday as priests, being the channel for God's interaction with the world.[3]

Though there are tensions between a gospel of grace and a competitive world of profit and high consumption, Diehl portrays how the Christian faith equips persons for doing good work, gaining "enough" to have a comfortable, though not excessive lifestyle, and seeks ways to help more people have decent jobs and income. The worship and ministries of our congregations depend on those who give their time, talents, and gifts for the "work of the church", but the real mission of the church is *to help equip and form disciples to do their "work in the world."* This is what I am calling the "integrity thing": responding to the situations and people of our life out of our relationship with God instead of reacting to them all on our own.

More recently, I happened to come across two books that I read back to back—*Reclaiming the Fire* and *Nickel and Dimed*. In *Reclaiming the Fire: How Successful People Overcome Burnout*, psychologist Steven Berglas describes some of the burnout and career meltdowns that sometimes occur with highly successful and competent people. Using Michael Jordan's early retirement and later return to professional basketball as an example, Berglas portrays what he calls *supernova burnout*: "A psychological disorder that results when a competent person who is, or could be, successful in a professional arena experiences a state of chronic trepidation, distress, despondency, or depression attributable to the belief that he is trapped in a job, or on a career path, from which he can neither escape nor derive psychological gratification."[4]

Some of the other malaises of the successful that Dr. Berglas explores are what he intriguingly names *success depression, encore anxiety,* and *entrepre-*

neurial arson. Achieving what we set out for may not be all it's cracked up to be, leaving us with an 'is this all there is?' feeling. Those who do well can become burdened by fear they can't sustain their success or do it again. And there are times when high achievers may consciously or unconsciously sabotage themselves to get out of the seemingly rat-race situation. All of these represent a kind of frantic reacting in contrast to a centered response.

Whereas Berglas examines the dilemmas of those on top of the success-economic world, Barbara Ehrenreich views matters from the bottom. In *Nickel and Dimed: On (Not) Getting By in America*, Ehrenreich tells of her experiences of "going underground" and working in an array of near minimum wage jobs to see if people get by at that level, and if so, how. Over the course of a year, Ehrenreich worked as a waitress, as a housecleaning service maid, a nursing home aide, and a Wal-Mart associate. Overall, she found the employee benefits meager to non-existent, the hours wearying, relentless pressure from management to go along and not make waves, and the pay barely able to cover food, housing, and transportation, if at all. She writes:

> In orientation, we learned that the store's success depends entirely on us, the associates; in fact, our bright blue vests bear the statement "At Wal-Mart, our people make the difference." Underneath those vests, though, there are real-life charity cases, maybe even shelter dwellers.[5]

Between the top and bottom of the socioeconomic ladder is where the majority of us find ourselves, with our daily mix of peaks, valleys, and monotonous middles. Indeed, someone has suggested that we are no longer in a time of "career ladders" but now in an era of "career lattices." Few stay in the same job or even field for forty years anymore. With a variety of jobs and professions across the years, the challenge arises for us to have a sense of wholeness, integrity, and call about our lives.

Without glossing over the unfinished business of fairness and equity in our society's job, wage, and benefit practices, I want to share some "ministries" I have gleaned from observation and study. From top to bottom to middle jobs, these ministries can bring integrity and meaning to the work we do.

The Ministry of Competence

In a world of shoddy work and shortcuts, there are some people who do their work well. I mentioned earlier my friend the car mechanic who practices the life-saving work of what I call brake ministry. For a fair price, he does good work that provides income for him and his employees, and literally saves the lives of people in and around my cars. I also appreciate my insurance agent. He, too, is a church going person, who lives out his faith with the ministry of competence. For sure he is making a living and a commission on my account, yet I appreciate how over the years he has helped me make sure our family is as secure as it can be now and later in an uncertain world.

Ehrenreich was moved by those beleaguered minimum income workers who still exhibited some pride and care in their work. She observes, "While I encountered some cynics and plenty of people who had learned to budget their energy, I never met an actual slacker or, for that matter, a drug addict or thief. On the contrary, I was amazed and sometimes saddened by the pride people took in jobs that rewarded them so meagerly, either in wages or in recognition."[6]

The Ministry of Showing Up

Using a phrase from Gaylord Noyce, Yale Professor of Pastoral Theology, this ministry can also be called "the ministry of chipping away." Most days, people don't find the miracle cure, make a bundle in business, or wipe out evil once and for all. But most days, there are a host of faithful people who put one foot in front of the other and show up for work, for volunteer service, with people who need them and little by little chip away, making the world a little bit better. In his book *The Minister as Moral Counselor*, Professor Noyce states:

> This chipping away is the Christian calling, not the realization of a moral utopia. It is important to put the matter in these terms because, lacking this understanding, a morally serious person may find the impossibility of moral innocence or large-scale reform to be devastating. He or she may end up callous, or . . . evolving toward the cynical view that moral concerns stop at the

102

workplace door. Chipping away means righting wrongs where possible, enhancing the moral quality of workplace community, and reaching for the larger innovations and reforms as the occasion arises.[7]

When it comes to the mighty ministers of chipping away in our society, public school teachers are my heroes. Teachers have the almost impossible task of not only teaching children reading, writing, and arithmetic, they also midwife the emerging personalities and coach the interpersonal relation skills of their charges. Society struggles with racial inclusiveness, male/female roles, socioeconomic inequities, healthcare coverage, TV media's sex and violence content, and family structure volatility. Our teachers deal with the products and consequences of all this each day in their students. Usually in under-funded schools with too little or too much parental involvement, teachers are the front line in the effort to form the next generation. At the present time, children still do not come equipped with little video screens across their foreheads that report: "It may not look like it, but you are getting through to me. I don't realize it now, but some day I will appreciate you." Yet we, our children, and grandchildren are beneficiaries of the chipping away ministry of teachers who have heard and been faithful to their call.

In a church I served, I preached a sermon that was about how all of us have a ministry in our work and life, that our jobs can be ways we serve God through the quality of our work and our relationships with our colleagues and customers. Karen (not her real name) sought me out to talk. She had begun participating in the church about six months before, quickly joined the choir, and was noticed by a number of us as the one who always smiled when she sang like she really enjoyed it. Karen shared that she was touched and disturbed by my sermon on work as ministry. It turned out that she was a "trailer park," single parent who juggled three part-time jobs to support herself and her first grader, who had his share of health and learning problems. She did this with little to no help from her former husband, their child's father, who lived several states away and was many months behind on child support.

Though Karen did her work well and tried to treat people fairly, she felt trapped in what I would call "ratty" jobs. In a kind but direct way, she let me know that what I had said had not helped, but instead had made her feel even more cut off from doing anything that mattered or had meaning. As she talked, I was struck by the quality of her life and the gritty integrity she had as she did what she had to do to care for herself and the child who depended on her. I struggled to express my deep appreciation and admiration for the way she was being a faithful person in hard circumstances. Though she certainly could not buy groceries or go to the bank with my word of encouragement, I tried hard to affirm her valiant chipping away ministry. In time, some people in our church helped Karen connect with a better job and some junior college courses. Karen reminds me that there are probably a lot more, not less, people out there "chipping away." A "ratty" job in the service of those who depend on you *is* a ministry—maybe not at the cash register, but certainly in taking care of your children.

The Ministry of Encouragement

The root word for "courage" is *coeur*, which is French for "heart." Many days, many of us are trying to go on with our lives without losing heart. We are tired, wondering if anyone notices or cares, questioning if what we do matters after all, and trying to stay on track despite our particular set of problems and predicaments nibbling away our energy and confidence. While serving as District Superintendent, I found that although many pastors operate daily as "professional encouragers" to others, they themselves can sometimes feel a bit taken for granted and unnoticed by their parishioners and the Conference (bishop, superintendent, and peers).

From a gentle touch, pat on the back, squeeze of the hand, to a nod, smile, or wink, gestures of encouragement help. Encouragement communications include phone calls, emails, cards, notes, a quick visit, or an "atta boy/you go girl" compliment. These are little things that can mean a lot. In a microwave, fast food culture, I even know a few folks who will show up at your door with a cake or casserole. I call the skillful practitioners of the ministry of encouragement "faithful noticers."

A while back, late on a hot summer afternoon, after one of those days, I came home and reported to my wife that I was going for a run. When she protested that it was too hot, I said that I needed to go out and get so hot and out of breath that I couldn't think about anything but being hot and out of breath, and thus take my mind off my frustrations. I set out on my run. About halfway through, I was fading fast and considering stopping and walking back home. About that time I came upon a carpenter loading up his tools in the back of his pickup after a day at a building site. As I huffed and puffed by, he called out with a grin: "Hey, you're looking good! Keep it up!"

Well, I was *not* looking good, and his words were likely a good-natured way of making fun of my plodding plight. Or maybe it was another tired guy's way of saying, "I see you and affirm what you are doing." Maybe it was just a playful quip given without any deep meaning on his part. Whatever it was, it helped. I don't exactly know what happened. Perhaps one human being's encouraging words somehow can trigger another's endorphins, but I picked it up and felt a bit of a second wind. Humor helps. Encouragement helps. It's a ministry we all need and one we all can do.

The Ministry of Seeing Jesus' Face

Mother Teresa, the Albanian nun who based her work with the poor of Calcutta, was often asked how she did it. How does one day after day hold, wash, and feed undernourished, sick, and often dying throwaway people off the streets? The answer that Mother Teresa gave was that she saw Jesus' face in each of these faces.

That brings to mind Jesus' great parable of the last judgment in Matthew 25. His message was how we treat or fail to treat seemingly insignificant persons is as if we are doing it to him. Some might take this as a parable of threat: if you treat even the most seemingly unimportant person badly, it will catch up with you. Maybe so. More important is that it is a parable of promise: the seemingly insignificant acts between us are of great significance, even having holy mysterious meaning: As we seek to be Christ-like to others, they are Christ with us.

Still, let's be honest. To see Jesus' face in the sweet and meek, in the appropriately cooperative and appreciative people around us, is not much of an accomplishment. But to seek and see Jesus' face in the people whose lives are a wreck, or even harder, to see that face in the people who are jerks who cause complications in our lives, is easier said than done. Here, we clearly depend on God's grace, that gives us the ability to do what we never could on our own. To respond to people out of an awareness of their and our relationship with God and not to react out of our own insecurity and self-promoting is an exquisite exercise in applied integrity.

Several years ago, some friends and I spent the day in conversation with spiritual director and author Flora Wuellner. With her kind, round face crowned with a swirl of every-which-a-way salt-and-pepper hair, she talked with us about people in our lives who seem to have a way of draining our energy. I have heard such people called "energy drainers", even "energy vampires." These people, Flora reminded us, could be loved ones whose needs and expectations of us can leave us fatigued and frustrated. "It is as if," she said, "whatever help or energy we give them in direct proportion depletes us." Flora suggested a practice that I see as a variation of seeing Jesus' face. When the "energy drainers" come, imagine a lifeline like those attached to astronauts as they explore outside their spaceships coming down from heaven to you and to the other person. The point of the exercise is to remind ourselves that all the energy we have comes from God, not us, and there is plenty for all. Whatever help we might be is not an energy transfer from me to you or you to me, but to both of us from God.

The Ministries of Competence, Showing Up, Chipping Away, Encouragement, and Seeing Jesus' Face are patterns of living made possible by the power of God's grace. We should be careful not to reduce them to little more than positive attitude gimmicks. What's more, even a good job can have "ratty" days. And on a deeper note, we cannot forget that meaningful work with decent pay and adequate benefits continues to be a systemic matter before us as a society and requires appropriate Christian citizenship efforts in the political and economic community. Yet these ministries do allow us the gift of an occasional gritty integrity that connects how we do our work and treat people to the God who is the source of all good works and gifts.

I'm Still Receiving It

In *God Underneath: Spiritual Memoirs of a Catholic Priest*, Edward Beck tells of his struggle and decision to become a priest. His experience was something like that of Barbara Brown Taylor's. Coming to understand that being a priest was finally not something God demanded of him but something God invited him to do made his decision more satisfying.

> I used to think if I hadn't become a priest, God would be mad at me, or at least disappointed. I don't think that anymore. I think I could have chosen to be a truck driver and God would have been just fine with it (my mother, I'm not sure about). Don't get me wrong. I think God is happy that I've chosen to do this with my life, but something else may have been just as tickling. The requisite is my happiness and my ability to contribute to the happiness of others. I think that's what gets God to do back flips. HOW that happens is relatively immaterial to God.[8]

Beck's words help recap what has been explored in this chapter on Integrity and our Life Work. (1) God's call to ministry is not a heavy burden we have *got to* do by God's demand but something we *get to* do by God's grace. (2) You don't have to be a minister to be a minister. (Though we need more pastors!) We delight in the ministry of all Christians: the ones who really get God's work done in the world. Of such, there are the ministries to teaching, business, medicine, car mechanics, mail delivery; fill in your own blank. By baptism, every Christian is called to be in ministry for Jesus Christ.

Edward Beck, again: "'When did you receive your calling?' is a question I am asked. I like to respond, 'I'm still receiving it.'"[9]

Our call to be a minister of Jesus, somehow a channel of God's love for others, through our lifework, pastor-wise or otherwise, is not a one-time event shrinking ever smaller in the rearview mirror of our memory. Our calling is a dimension of our integrity, a dynamic part of our ongoing relationship with God, and the ways we respond to our lives (work, people, and commitments) in light of that fundamental relationship. At every point along the way in our lives, we discover anew what it means to be a minister, to have a calling, in our particular set of circumstances and web of relationships. As a District Superintendent with responsibilities for some fifty churches and seventy pastors, I lived my calling differently than I do now that I am a local church pastor again. In the same way, as a parent of adult children, I live my calling in relation to them differently than when they were little.

Beck writes, "The calling is to fullness of life and to facilitating fullness of life. The call by the lake that Simon and Andrew received from Jesus was a call to discipleship, to be 'fishers of men and women.' All of us receive the same call today, no matter how we choose to live it."[10]

Early in my ministry, I heard a story that is likely a blend of fact and fiction, yet whatever the facts of the story, its truth is self-authenticating.

> Long ago, in a great European cathedral, there was a majestic pipe organ. The instrument was of such priceless value one of the monk's sole responsibility was the care and protection of it. One day when the church was pretty much empty, a stranger showed up, approached the old monk, told him he had always heard of the great organ, and asked to play it. After refusing the stranger's repeated and increasingly intense requests, the monk gave in, giving him just a few moments to play and strongly cautioning him to be ever so careful with the precious instrument. The stranger played the organ more beautifully than the monk had heard in all his years; the whole cathedral was filled with the exquisite music. With eyes brimming, the monk asked, "Who are you?" The stranger answered, "I am Johann Sebastian Bach." "Mein Gott!" gasped the old man. "To think that I almost refused to let the master use my instrument!"

The instrument is, of course, our lives. Saying that our life's work has *got to* be a calling does not quite express it fully. Discovering that our lives *get to* be a calling does.

Reflections for Spiritual Formation

Reflection One

Reflect on the twenty-four hours just past. Write down the activities of your day. Draw a circle in your journal or on a blank page in this book. Now make a pie chart of the activities of the day, using the categories below:

    God

    Family

    Work (at home or away)

    Sleep

    Play or recreation

    Other activities

Where are you out of balance? What does this say about your relationship with God and with others? Where do you need to change? Write your responses in the space provided or in your journal.

_____

_____

_____

_____

_____

_____

Prayer

This prayer is attributed to humanitarian Dr. Albert Schweitzer (1875-1965):

> Here, Lord, is my life. I place it on the altar today. Use it as you will. Amen.

Reflection Two

In this chapter, the author tells us about using gifts at work. When we become members of the United Methodist Church, we pledge our prayers, presence, gifts, and service to the church and to God. Think about how can you employ your prayers, presence, gifts, and service on the job, whether in an office, hospital, classroom, home, or anywhere. Who in your life-work do you feel needs a prayer now? Write a prayer for that person.

_____

_____

_____

_____

Prayer

Lord, Work with Me

My God, since You are with me, and since it is Your will that I should apply my mind to these outward things, I pray that You will give me the grace to remain with You and keep company with You. But so that my work may be better, Lord, work with me; receive my work and possess all my affections. Amen.

Brother Lawrence (1611-1691)

The Practice of the Presence of God

Spire Books, p. 27

Reflection Three

Re-read and answer the questions the author poses on page 99. Answer them for yourself, writing your answers in the space provided.

_____

_____

_____

_____

_____

Now look at the four "ministries" the author describes on pages 102-105. Which of these four do you feel best answer the questions above? Why?

_____

_____

_____

_____

_____

_____

Now write a prayer of discernment, asking God to guide you to and help you in your "ministry."

_____

_____

_____

_____

_____

Prayer

O Lord, forgive what I have been, sanctify what I am, and order what I shall be.

Chapter Seven Notes

1. Barbara Brown Taylor, *The Preaching Life*, p. 27
2. Taylor, p. 23
3. William E. Diehl, *Thank God, It's Monday*, p. 89
4. Steven Berglas, *Reclaiming the Fire: How Successful People Overcome Burnout*, p. 19
5. Barbara Ehrenreich, *Nickel and Dimed: On (Not) Getting By In America*, p. 175
6. Ehrenreich, p. 212
7. Gaylord Noyce, *The Minister As Moral Counselor*, p. 114
8. Edward Beck, *God Underneath: The Spiritual Memoirs of a Catholic Priest*, p. 59
9. Beck, p. 59
10. Beck, p. 59

Unkillable Integrity

Eye has not seen, nor ear heard, nor the human heart conceived, what God has prepared for those who love him. (1 Corinthians 2:9)

In *Why I Am A United Methodist*, Bishop Will Willimon, former chaplain at Duke University, tells of a student who declared, "There's nothing worth dying for." About this, Dr. Willimon mused, "Which means one day she will have the unpleasant task of dying for nothing."[1]

Through the pages of this book and weeks of this study, we have explored integrity: A life that is whole, congruent, and aligned with firm values; a life that has discerned a pattern by which to live with honesty and compassion. None of us can set and sustain that course, that pattern, on our own. Thus, we have advanced a working definition of integrity as *responding to our lives in relationship to God instead of reacting to things on our own.* For people of Christian faith and life, integrity is finally not contained in a concept, definition or principle; it is embodied in a person. Whatever else Jesus was, he was and is the incarnation/enskinment of integrity. The pattern and power to live with joy, serve with love, and die with hope come from him.

Truth in advertising: Not everyone liked Jesus. Some loved him, but others loathed him. His life eventuated to a cross, the first-century version of lethal injection or the electric chair. His last week began with Jesus' hip-hooray-hosanna entry into Jerusalem. But by weekend, the parade had turned into a train wreck. Good (awful) Friday. Then drop dead Saturday. For his life of integrity (caring for people others wanted to write off, bringing God into the business of Monday instead of safety sequestered to Sunday/Sabbath) they did not give Jesus the key to the city of Jerusalem. They killed him.

In various ways, the fate of people of integrity continues to be daunting. Though even the best of leaders have flaws, those like Lincoln and Martin Luther King paid a mortal price for calling us to a life of integrity in human community before many were ready. Of late, corporate and government whistle blowers put themselves at considerable risk.

Though Christians have hope for more to life both before and after death, we need to recognize that a life of integrity may be rewarded with rugged consequences. What's more, there is a subtle lack of integrity if we use integrity or people as means for earthly recognition or heavenly reward.

Yet (the great yet) when it seemed clear that Jesus was just another dreamer who had valiantly tried, apparently in vain, to go against the greed and power systems of the world, something happened. When good sense said he was dead and gone, his followers experienced him alive and powerful among them. Something gave disciples, who had run away in fear, the courage to come back. Something mysterious, powerful, and wonderful happened. Those chicken hearts became brave hearts. They gave the rest of their lives to spread the good news of Jesus' passion for living, compassion for people, and hope for dying. A working definition for such hope is *a trust that God has more for our life both before and after we die than we can see just now.*

Barbara Brown Taylor writes:

> There is nothing in the gospel about being impressive or successful. There is nothing about being the biggest or best at anything at all. The good news of God in Christ is that when the bottom has fallen out from under you—when you have crashed through all your safety nets and you hear the bottom rushing up to meet you—the good news is that you cannot fall farther than God can catch you. You can't be too picky about where the catch happens, I'm afraid. Sometimes it happens after the funeral is over as it did with Jesus, but the good news he brought back to us can

never be revoked. God is stronger than death. Way past where we can see how it works, God is able to take our weakness, our fear, our trembling, and turn it into fullness of life.[2]

We consider the great "after words" of living and dying, which we cannot fully "wordify." In our efforts to live with integrity and compassion with each other, the Living Lord helps us see the truth that is deeper and wider than the limited logistics of our cerebral cubbyholes and synapsial swirlies .

In his message "The Weight of Glory," C. S. Lewis said: "There are no ordinary people. You have never talked to a mere mortal. Nations, cultures, arts, civilizations—these are mortal, and their life is to ours as the life of a gnat. But it is immortals whom we joke with, work with, marry, snub, and exploit—immortal horrors or everlasting splendours . . . . Next to the Blessed Sacrament itself, your neighbor is the holiest object presented to your senses."[3]

Near the end of his life, Methodist theologian-Wesleyan scholar Albert Outler framed an apt benediction-blessing, quoted in Bevel Jones' *One Step Beyond Caution*.[4]

"Hold fast to Christ, and for all the rest—hang loose!"

AFTERWORD NOTES

1. William Willimon, *Why I Am A United Methodist*, p. 51
2. Barbara Brown Taylor, *God In Pain: Teaching Sermons on Pain*, pp. 133-134
3. Alan Jacobs, *The Narnia: The Life and Times of C. S. Lewis*, p. 300
4. L. Bevel Jones III, *One Step Beyond Caution: Reflections on a Life and Faith*, p. 65

BIBLIOGRAPHY

Ayling, Stanley. *John Wesley*. New York: William Collins Publishers, 1979.

Bartlett, John. *Familiar Quotations: A collection of passages, phrases and proverbs traced to their sources in ancient and modern literature*. 15th and 125th Anniversary ed. Boston: Little, Brown and Company, 1980.

Beck, Edward. *God Underneath: Spiritual Memoirs of a Catholic Priest*. New York: Doubleday, 2001.

Berglas, Steven. *Reclaiming the Fire: How Successful People Overcome Burnout*. New York: Random House, 2001.

The Book of Discipline of the United Methodist Church. 2004 ed. Nashville: United Methodist Publishing House, 2004.

Davies, Robertson. *What's Bred in the Bone*. New York: Viking, 1985.

Davies, Rupert E., ed. *The Works of John Wesley: The Methodist Societies*. Vol. 9. Nashville: Abingdon, 1989.

Diehl, William. *Thank God, It's Monday*. Minneapolis: Augsburg, 1982.

Earle, Mary C. and Sylvia Maddox. *Holy Companions: Spiritual Practices from the Celtic Saints*. Harrisburg: Morehouse Publishing, 2004.

Ehrenreich, Barbara. *Nickel and Dimed: On (Not) Getting by in America*. New York: Metropolitan Books, 2001.

Friedman, Thomas. *The World is Flat*. New York: Farrar, Strauss, and Giroux, 2005.

Halberstam, David. *Summer of '49*. New York: W. Morrow, 1989.

Harris, Mark. *Companions for Your Spiritual Journey: Discovering the Disciplines of the Saints*. Downers Grove, IL: InterVarsity Press, 1999.

Jacobs, Alan. *The Narnian: The Life and Imagination of C. S. Lewis*. San Francisco: Harper Collins, 2005.

Johnson, Haynes. *The Best of Times: America in the Clinton Years*. New York: Harcourt, 2001.

Jones, L. Bevel, III. *One Step Beyond Caution: Reflections on Life and Faith*. Decatur, GA: Looking Glass Books, 2001.

Knight, Henry H., III. *The Presence of God in the Christian Life*. Metuchen, NJ: Scarecrow Press, 1992.

Lamott, Anne. *Traveling Mercies: Some Thoughts on Faith*. New York: Pantheon Books, 1999.

Lawrence, Brother. *The Practice of the Presence of God*. Old Tappan, NJ: Spire Books, 1958.

Lee, Harper. *To Kill a Mockingbird*. New York: Harper and Row, 1960.

The Legend of Bagger Vance. Dir. Robert Redford. DreamWorks Pictures, 2000.

Maddox, Randy L. *Responsible Grace: John Wesley's Practical Theology*. Nashville: Abingdon Press, 1994.

Marxsen, Willi. *New Testament Foundations for Christian Ethics*. Minneapolis: Fortress, 1993.

McElwain, Sarah, ed. *Saying Grace: Blessings for the Family Table*. San Francisco: Chronicle Books, 2003.

Moltmann, Jurgen. *Passion for Life: A Messianic Lifestyle*. Philadelphia: Fortress Press, 1978.

Mundy, Linus. *A Retreat with Desert Mystics: Thirsting for the Reign of God*. Cincinnati, OH: St. Anthony Press, 2000.

Outler, Albert C., ed. *The Works of John Wesley: Sermons I*. Vol. 1. Nashville: Abingdon, 1984.

Outler, Albert C., ed. *The Works of John Wesley: Sermons III*. Vol. 3. Nashville: Abingdon, 1986.

The New Interpreter's Bible: A Commentary in Twelve Volumes. Vol. IX. Nashville: Abingdon, 1995.

The New Oxford Annotated Bible. New Revised Standard Version. New York: Oxford University Press, 1991).

Niebuhr, H. Richard. *The Responsible Self*. New York: Harper, 1963.

Noyce, Gaylord. *The Minister as Moral Counselor*. Nashville: Abingdon, 1989.

Potok, Chaim. *In the Beginning*. New York: Knopf, 1975.

Rolheiser, Ronald. *The Shattered Lantern*. New York: Crossroad, 2001.

Runyon, Theodore. *The New Creation: John Wesley's Theology Today*. Nashville: Abingdon Press, 1998.

Sheldon, Charles M. *In His Steps*. New York: Putnam, 1984.

Signs. Dir. M. Night Shyamalan. Touchstone Pictures, 2002.

Taylor, Barbara Brown. *God in Pain*. Nashville: Abingdon, 1998.

———. *The Preaching Life*. Boston: Cowley, 1993).

Weems, Lovett. *The Gospel According to John Wesley*. Nashville: Discipleship Press, 1982.

———. *Leadership in the Wesleyan Spirit.* Nashville: Abingdon Press, 1999.

Wesley, John. *John Wesley's Forty-four Sermons.* London: Epworth Press, 1944.

———. *A Plain Account of Christian Perfection.* London: Epworth Press, 1968.

Willimon, William. *Why I am a United Methodist.* Nashville: Abingdon Press, 1990.

Wink, Walter. *Violence and Nonviolence in South Africa: Jesus' Third Way.* Philadelphia, PA: New Society Publishers, 1987.

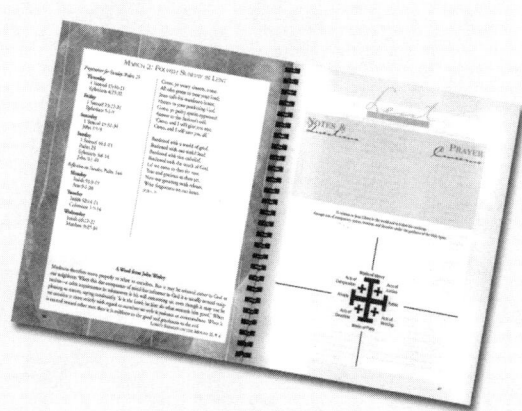